Venice

Text by Rob Hill

Berlitz POCKET GUIDE

Venice

Twelfth Edition 2003
Updated 2006

PHOTOGRAPHY BY:
8, 13, 22, 25, 26, 27, 29, 31, 34, 39, 40, 41, 43, 47, 51, 52, 53, 57, 59, 60, 63, 64, 68, 70, 71, 73, 75, 76, 82, 85, 89, 92, 97 Glyn Genin; 1, 30, 35, 61, 67, 72, 83, 94 Ros Miller; 6, 7, 9, 10, 44, 48, 54, 56, 79, 86, 98, 101 Chris Coe; 24, 81, 91, 99 Jon Davison; 93 Alessandra Santarelli; 37 Scala/Firenze; 14, 17 AKG; 18, 20 Topham Picturepoint; 84 Mary Evans Picture Library
Cover Photograph: Glyn Genin

CONTACTING THE EDITORS
Every effort has been made to provide accurate information in this publication, but changes are inevitable. The publisher cannot be responsible for any resulting loss, inconvenience or injury. We would appreciate it if readers would call our attention to any errors or outdated information by contacting Berlitz Publishing, PO Box 7910, London SE1 1WE, England. Fax: (44) 20 7403 0290;
e-mail: berlitz@apaguide.co.uk
www.berlitzpublishing.com

◄ Former home of the Venetian rulers, the Palazzo Ducale (page 34) overlooks San Marco and the lagoon

► See Tintoretto's splendid work at the Scuola Grande di San Rocco (page 62)

◄ The iconic Santa Maria della Salute (page 53) is a familiar landmark on the lagoon

The Bridge of Sighs (page 38) links the Palazzo Ducale with the city's former jail ◄

TOP TEN ATTRACTIONS

The Grand Canal (page 64), lined with Renaissance palaces, is the city's spectacular main waterway

The Rialto (page 57), the historic heart of Venice's commercial quarter, is still famed for its markets

The island of Murano (page 78) is world renowned for its long tradition of glassmaking

At the heart of Venice is the Basilica di San Marco (page 29), its belltower and vast piazza

The Accademia (page 48) showcases Venetian painting from the 14th to 18th centuries

For modern art visit the Collezione Peggy Guggenheim (page 51)

CONTENTS

A ➤ in the text denotes a highly recommended sight

INTRODUCTION

Venice, the jewel of the Adriatic, is one of a kind. For an unbroken 1,100 years, it was an independent empire and a republic, with a constitution that is studied and admired by students of politics to this day. In the 9th century, while the majority of Europe's cities were hidden behind defensive walls, Venice stood open to the world, protected only by its lagoon. A tantalizing blend of East and West, it was neither totally European nor wholly Italian. Traces of Byzantium and more exotic Asian influences are apparent everywhere.

From a distance the city is a fantasy of sumptuous buildings that seem to float on the surface of the Adriatic. And once you walk its narrow streets *(calli)* or glide along its canals, you cannot fail to be moved by the graceful, exotically romantic architecture that has inspired artists and travellers alike for centuries. While most other great cities have been scarred with main roads and high-rise blocks, Venice remains unsullied by modernity, looking virtually as it did in its heyday, three centuries ago.

Geography

Decorative Venetian mask

Situated at the northwestern end of the Adriatic Sea, Venice lies on an archipelago in a crescent-shaped lagoon 50 km (32 miles) in length. At just 1 metre (3¼ft) above sea-level, Greater Venice stands on 118 flat islets, with its buildings supported by millions of larch poles driven into sediment. Crisscrossing

Gondoliers on a break

the city is a labyrinth of over 160 canals, spanned by more than 600 bridges. These canals are partly flushed out by the tides that sweep in daily from the Adriatic through three seaways that pierce the ring of sand bars *(lidi)* protecting the lagoon.

The Adriatic

The sea has always been linked with the city's fortunes and, like the swampy, shallow Venetian lagoon, it is loved as if it were part of the city itself. However, with rising sea levels and subsidence caused by falling water tables, Venice has been increasingly swept by flood tides each winter *(see page 11)*. After many years of debate, construction of the MOSE tidal barrier is now underway. The 79 steel flood gates will close the three lagoon inlets when severe floods are forecast. The project is opposed by environmentalists, who argue that the barrier will destroy the delicate ecological balance of the lagoon, to which Venice owes its existence.

Negotiating the City

Any visitor to Venice has to confront its unique geography. To explore the city properly, you have to be prepared to pound the streets – in fact, this is a pleasure in such a car-free environment – and to climb the many bridges that span the canals. This is not a city to visit with excess baggage, as most travellers will at some point have to carry their luggage through sometimes crowded, narrow pedestrian streets and over bridges to their hotels.

When walking becomes tiring, take to the water aboard a *vaporetto* (waterbus). The main *vaporetto* lines ply the Grand Canal, but the system will also take you out to the far corners of the Venetian lagoon – from the beaches at the Lido and the brightly painted houses of the island of Burano to the wall-to-wall glass showrooms and factories on Murano and the medieval cathedral set amid the salt meadows on the island of Torcello.

For and Against Tourism

Tourism has become both the lifeblood and the bane of Venice, with around 12 million tourists spending at least one day in the city each year. This is nothing new: in his novella *Death in Venice*, Thomas Mann describes the city as 'half fairy tale, half tourist trap'. Visitors seem to be stung financially at every turn: hotel prices are high by most standards, tourists pay higher fares than residents for use of the *vaporetti*, and restaurants around Piazza San Marco

Water marker

Bucolic Burano

and the other main tourist haunts charge grossly inflated prices for food and drink.

And it isn't just the tourists who suffer. In summer the city becomes so packed that it is difficult for everyone to negotiate the narrow streets near Piazza San Marco. The Venetians have become so overwhelmed by the tourist influx, and the city's infrastructure so overburdened by the hordes that there are plans either to limit the number of day-trippers entering the city each day, or to charge admission to visitors who enter without hotel reservations.

Avoiding the Crowds

Yet surcharges and a little extra physical effort are small prices to pay to wander this remarkable place, and if you explore beyond the central area around San Marco, you'll find peaceful neighbourhoods that show the Venice of the Venetians – areas with quirky shops and fairly priced restaurants, cafés and wine bars. This is not to diminish the pleasures of Piazza San Marco, which is undoubtedly one of the world's most beautiful squares, nor its wonderous Basilica and magnificent Palazzo Ducale – even at the height of the season, you can see these sights without being jostled, by simply visiting early or late in the day, when day-trippers are out of the equation.

The Venetians

In its heyday, the city of Venice had 200,000 inhabitants – a figure that fell to 90,000 at the end of the Republic and currently stands at around a mere 64,000. This emigration has not been wholly voluntary: the city has very little rented accommodation, and flats are too expensive for most locals to buy. Building restoration costs in Venice are also almost double those of mainland Mestre, from where many former Venetians, especially the younger generation, now commute.

In general, the Venetians are friendly, immensely hospitable and well versed in their city's treasures, although they can often be a little patronising towards anyone 'unfortunate enough' to have been born somewhere else. Their somewhat obscure dialect emphasizes the isolation of Venice. Visitors are often confused by the names of canals or districts spelled varyingly in Italian and Venetian. When asked directions, Venetians are fond of replying, 'Do you want the shortest way, or the beautiful way?' In Venice, however, there is no unattractive way.

Venice in Peril

Following disastrous floods in 1966, local and international organisations were set up to restore buildings and works of art in the city and to bring Venice's plight to world attention. At that time the city was actually sinking – a problem caused by the industrial complex of Porto Marghera drawing millions of gallons of lagoon water. That issue has begun to be addressed, but other massive problems remain, and the increasing regularity of the city's winter *aqua alta* (high-water flooding) is a symptom of this.

After years of bureaucratic wrangling, the MOSE flood barrier system is now under construction. Due for completion in 2011, it has been criticised as a short-term solution that ignores environmental concerns.

A BRIEF HISTORY

It may be hard to believe, but this tiny city was once the centre of the wealthiest, most powerful state in Europe. In its prime, Venice influenced the course of modern history, leaving an incomparable legacy in the shape of the city itself.

Early Venetians

Although the earliest Venetians were fishermen and boatmen skilled at navigating the shallow lagoon's islands, the first major settlers arrived after the Lombards invaded in AD568.

> When St Mark's relics reached Venice *c.*829, a chapel (the original St Mark's) was built for them next to the Palazzo Ducale. Mark's winged lion emblem was adopted as the symbol of the city.

This Barbarian onslaught caused the coastal dwellers to flee to low-lying offshore islands in the lagoon, such as Torcello and Malamocco, on the string of *lidi*, or barrier beaches, on the Adriatic.

Venetia, or Venezia, was the name of the entire area at the northern end of the Adriatic under the Roman empire. Venice as we know it developed gradually around a cluster of small islands that remained out of reach of the north Italian Lombard kingdom and were subject only to loose control from the Roman-Byzantine centre at Ravenna, which answered to Constantinople. Around AD697 the lagoon communities were united under a separate military command, set up at Malamocco, with a *dux* (Latin for leader), or doge, in charge. Though the first doges were probably selected by the lagoon dwellers, they still took orders from the Byzantine emperor.

The Lombards were succeeded on the mainland in 774 by Charlemagne's Frankish army, and in 810 his son Pépin was sent to conquer the communities of the lagoon. Pépin seized

the outer island of Mala-
mocco, but the doge and his
entourage managed to escape
to the safety of the Rivo Alto
(High Shore), the future
Rialto, where they built a
fortress on the site now
housing the Palazzo Ducale
(Doge's Palace).

The Rise of the Republic

The new city gradually became independent of distant
Byzantium, prospering due
to tight control of the north
Italian river deltas and, later,

Venetian and Italian flags

of the sea itself. Fishing, salt and the lumber and slave trades
enriched the city, and rival producers and traders were ruth-
lessly quashed. From the 9th century, in defiance of the pope
and the Byzantine emperor, the Venetians traded with the
Islamic world, selling luxuries from Constantinople at a high
profit to the rest of Europe. By this time, Venice was no
longer a dependency of the Byzantine Empire, and, to under-
line this, snatched the body of St Mark from Muslim-
controlled Alexandria, in Egypt, *c.*829. Mark replaced the
Byzantine saint, Theodore, as the patron of Venice.

Empire Building

The city's newly founded Arsenale turned out fleets of ever-
mightier galleys, enabling Venice to move into the Adriatic,
where it warred for decades with its bitter enemy, the Dalmatia. In the year 1000, the Republic scored a significant victory
and celebrated it with a 'marriage to the sea' ceremony,
which is still re-enacted annually *(see page 95)*. Ships flying

Bellini's portrait of Doge Loredan

St Mark's pennant ranged over the Aegean Sea and the eastern Mediterranean, trading, plundering and bringing back spoils to strengthen the state. Venice soon came to be known as the *Serenissima* (Most Serene Republic), or 'Queen of the Seas'.

From the start of the Crusades in 1095, the Venetians sensed rich pickings. Ideally positioned both politically and geographically between Europe and the East, and with little concern for the spiritual aspect of the campaigns, Venice produced and outfitted ships and equipped knights, often at huge profit.

In 1204 crusader armies, under the 90-year-old Doge Enrico Dandalo sacked Constantinople, the greatest repository of the ancient world's treasures; among the rich pickings shipped to Venice were four bronze horses that adorn the Basilica di San Marco. By now the Republic was a world power, controlling all the major points along the routes to Egypt and the Crimea.

At the end of the 13th century, the Venetians curbed the power of the doges, evolving into a patrician oligarchy. Eventually, the doges became little more than pampered prisoners in their palace, stripped of every vestige of authority; their primary function was to preside over the Republic's pompous festivities, and after 1310 no major change was made in the constitution until the Republic fell in 1797.

Wars and Intrigue

Venice spent much of the 14th century battling with its rival, Genoa, over the slave and grain trades in the Black Sea. They also fought over the route from the Mediterranean north to Bruges and Antwerp, where spices and other wares could be traded for prized Flemish cloth, English wool and tin. In 1379, during the fourth and final Genoese War, Venice came closer to defeat than at any time in its history: the Genoese fleet, aided by Hungarian and Paduan troops, captured and sank Venetian ships in home waters. When the key port of Chioggia, south of Venice, was taken, the *Serenissima* seemed lost. The Venetians retook the port, however, and in 1380 Genoa surrendered, forever finished as a major maritime force.

The 14th century was also a time for domestic difficulties. In 1310 a group of disgruntled aristocrats under Baiamonte Tiepolo tried to seize power and kill the doge, but their revolt was quickly crushed. Worse was to come: between 1347 and 1349 almost half of the city's population of 120,000 was wiped out by the Black Death. A further 20,000 Venetians died in another epidemic in 1382, and over the next three centuries the city was almost never free of plague.

Marco Polo

Venice's most famous citizen opened the eyes of 13th-century Europe to the irresistibly exotic mysteries of Asia. While recent scholarship has thrown some doubt on the authenticity of his story, Marco Polo relates how, for some 20 years, he served the Mongol emperor Kublai Khan and was the first Westerner permitted to travel about freely in China. When he came back from China, legend has it that no-one recognized him or believed his tales – until he slit the seams of his clothes and precious jewels fell out.

The Republic began to focus attention on its land boundary. As an expanding manufacturing city in the 15th century, it needed food, wood and metal from the nearest possible sources. However, its push along the northern Italian rivers and across the plain of Lombardy soon met with opposition, and the conflicts known as the Lombard Wars began in 1425. The Republic defended its new territory so tenaciously that Milan, Florence and Naples formed an anti-Venice coalition, worried that Venice might take over the entire Italian peninsula.

New Threats in a Golden Age

With the dying Byzantine Empire no longer able to buffer Venice against threats from the east, a new rival arose in the shape of the Ottoman Empire. Initially, the young sultan, Mohammed the Conqueror, was not taken seriously, and inadequate forces were sent by the Venetians to protect Constantinople. In 1453 the city fell to the Turks, who played havoc with Venetian trade routes and won a key naval battle at Negroponte in the northern Aegean in 1470. Although Venice was still the leading Mediterranean maritime power, these defeats marked the beginning of a downhill slide.

While its fortunes beyond the lagoon waned, Venetian civilisation reached new heights. No building in the Western world was more sumptuous than the Palazzo Ducale; no church had as many treasures as San Marco. And as artists such as Bellini, Giorgione, Carpaccio, Tintoretto, Veronese and Titian flourished, Andrea Palladio's revolutionary concepts began to shape the future of architecture. Venice was also home to the most complex economy and the richest culture in all Europe.

Yet the threats to the Republic continued to accumulate. In 1498 Vasco da Gama of Portugal undertook his epic voyage around the Cape of Good Hope to India, thus opening up new trade routes and putting an end to Venice's spice-trade

View of the Ducal Palace in Venice (c.1755) by Canaletto

monopoly. During the same period of prodigious exploration, Christopher Columbus's landfalls on the other side of the Atlantic proved momentous for the Venetian Republic. The axis of power in Europe gradually moved to countries on the Atlantic coast. As trade with the New World mushroomed, the Oriental trade that had long ensured Venetian prosperity fell into decline.

Decline and Decadence

After the French invasion of Italy in 1494, Venice sought to further encroach on the latter. However, this international brinkmanship so incensed the rest of Europe that, in 1508, under the auspices of Pope Julius II and the king of Spain, a pan-European organisation, known as the League of Cambrai, was formed with the aim of destroying the Republic. City after city defected, as the Republic's 20,000-strong mercenary army fell apart. For a while things seemed desperate,

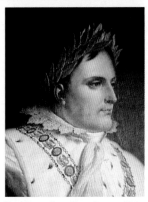

Napoleon, champion of a new Italy

but the League itself fell apart through internal struggles, and Venice managed to regain nearly all its territories. However, seven years of war cost the Venetians dearly, putting a stop to their ambitions in Italy. Furthermore, with Charles V's empire steadily accumulating Italian ground, considerable Venetian diplomacy was needed for the city to preserve its independence.

Around the eastern and southern Mediterranean, the Ottomans surged on, and the Battle of Lepanto, in 1571, finally turned the Turkish tide. The fleet of the Holy League was spearheaded by Venice, but the allies, by now suspicious of Venice, ensured that the city did not profit from this victory; instead of continuing the offensive east, they signed away the Venetian stronghold of Cyprus as part of the peace treaty.

From 1575 to 1577 plague raged again, and the populace fell from 150,000 to 100,000. Despite this, and the Republic's diminishing political powers, Venice prospered through the 16th and 17th centuries, aided by the skills and contacts of Jewish refugees from the Italian peninsula and Spain. Music flourished, with Claudio Monteverdi in the 17th century and Antonio Vivaldi in the 18th. Venice's art tradition continued with Tiepolo and Canaletto, and the playwright Carlo Goldoni's new adaptations of *commedia dell'arte* broke exciting theatrical ground. If the city was a fading world power, it fast warmed to its new role as the playground of Europe, staging extravagant carnival balls and becoming notorious for its gambling.

The End of the Republic

By the end of the 18th century the Venetians knew that Napoleon was on the war path but were simply too weak to stop him. He entered the city, demanding that the government turn its power over to a democratic council under French military protection. In 1797 the last doge, Ludovico Manin, abdicated, the Great Council voted to dissolve itself, and the *Serenissima* was no more.

Napoleon's troops looted and destroyed the Arsenale, but they stayed in Venice for only five months, until their emperor was forced to relinquish it to Austrian control. However, in 1805, Napoleon returned, having defeated the Austrians at Austerlitz, and he made the city part of his short-lived Kingdom of Italy.

After Waterloo, the Austrians again occupied Venice, and stayed for more than 50 years, until 1866. Although the Austrians were despised by the Venetians, they did restore to the city most of the artistic booty taken by Napoleon. In 1846 they linked Venice to the mainland for the first time, erecting an unsightly railway bridge.

In 1848, the Venetians rose up under revolutionary leader Daniele Manin and ousted the Austrian garrison; however, their provisional republic fell the following year. In 1866, after Austria's defeat by Prussia, the Venetians voted overwhelmingly in a referendum to join the new Kingdom of Italy, and eventually became the capital of one of the peninsula's 20 regions.

> Until the late 17th century the Palazzo Ducale was the only building in Venice that was allowed to be called a *palazzo*. Other splendid mansions were called simply Casa (house), shortened to Ca'. Many families did not bother to rename their houses *palazzi* once it was permitted, hence Ca' d'Oro, Ca' da Mosto and so on.

Prime Minister Silvio Berlusconi

The City Today

Although Venice remained virtually untouched by the two world wars, it was not without its troubles in the 20th century. The construction of a large commercial harbour and oil refinery at Porto Marghera in the 1920s and 1930s caused significant pollution problems. By tapping the region's water table, it created both flooding and sinking conditions and provoked a harmful build-up of algae. Since disastrous flooding in November 1966, when the city was flooded for 13 hours up to a depth of nearly 2m (over 6ft), the Venetians and the international community have been stirred into action to save and revive the city's ancient fabric. In 1992 the Italian government released funds for the controversial construction of huge mobile flood protection barriers at the Porto di Lido, Porto di Malamocco and Porto di Chioggia. However, after a viability study by a team of international experts, the project, known as MOSE (or 'Moses'), was put on hold by the government at the end of 1998 and only finally given the go-ahead in 2001.

Paradoxically, the biggest problem nowadays is also the city's most lucrative trade – tourism. At peak season, a daily influx of more than 25,000 tourists takes its toll on the city's fragile infrastructure and threatens to destroy the very sights they have come to admire. Tighter control over the number of visitors, together with strict measures to counter the risk of flooding, control pollution and reverse the exodus of the young population are all issues that must be addressed to enable the city to face the future with confidence.

Historical Landmarks

6th century AD Refugees fleeing barbarians settle in the lagoon.

696 Election of Paoluccio Anafesto as the first doge.

828 The body of St Mark, stolen from Alexandria, is smuggled to Venice.

991–1008 Doge Pietro Orseolo II reigns. Commercial advantages are gained from Byzantium, and a sea battle is won against Dalmatia.

1104 The Arsenale is founded.

1202–4 Venice diverts the Fourth Crusade and sacks Constantinople.

1380 War with Genoa ends in a Venetian victory at Chioggia.

1405 Venice takes Verona from Milan.

1423 Election of Doge Francesco Foscari begins Venetian expansion to Bergamo and Brescia and on to parts of Cremona.

1453 The Turks take Constantinople, heralding the expansion of the Ottoman Empire in Europe.

1498 Vasco da Gama reaches the East Indies, marking the beginning of the end for Venice's spice monopoly.

1508 The League of Cambrai against Venice results in territorial losses.

1571 Resounding victory against the Turks at Lepanto.

1797 Napoleonic troops enter Venice, and the Republic comes to an end.

1815 The Treaty of Vienna places the Veneto under Austrian control.

1848 Under Daniele Manin, Venice rebels against Austria.

1866 Venice becomes part of unified Italy.

1914–18 World War I. More than 600 bombs are dropped on Venice.

1920s/1930s Commercial harbour and oil refinery built at Marghera.

1966 Disastrous flooding leads to the launch of an international appeal.

1994 Approval of MOSE, a mobile dam designed to prevent flooding.

1995 Fiftieth anniversary of the Biennale.

1996–7 The most severe floods for 30 years; fire at La Fenice opera house.

2002 The euro replaces the Italian lira as the country's unit of currency.

2004 La Fenice reopens. The use of broadband is introduced across the city, ridding Venice of unsightly satellite dishes.

2005 Berlusconi gives the go ahead for the second phrase of the controversial MOSE project. Protesters attempt to halt work on the barriers.

WHERE TO GO

The incomparable *palazzi*, canals and lagoons of Venice (Venezia) present something of a fantasy world, even to the most seasoned of travellers. At times of winter floods, Carnival shenanigans or the peak of summer, when tourists descend en masse, the myth may seem at risk of turning into a nightmare; yet even at these hectic times you can still take refuge in a café once frequented by Casanova or a quiet alley that looks just as it did 400 years ago. A great bonus in Venice is the absence of cars – it's a rare joy to be able to wander around a town without battling with road traffic or breathing in petrol fumes. Stand on a little humpbacked bridge, far from the Grand Canal, and all you'll hear will be the water lapping against the mossy walls, or the swish of a gondola that appears out of nowhere.

Don't try to see the city in a day. Without sufficient time to meander and explore its hidden corners, you risk seeing little more than Piazza San Marco and hence failing to understand the city's inherent charm. A useful way to orientate yourself is to divide the city into four: southeast (San Marco and Castello), south and southwest (Dorsoduro), central (San Polo and Santa Croce) and north (Cannaregio). As you wander, you'll find some walls on major thoroughfares marked with signs that indicate the way to the Rialto, Piazzale Roma, Piazza San Marco, the Accademia and specific tourist attractions, as well as ACTV *(vaporetto)* and *traghetto* (gondola ferry) stations.

> **Visit Venice in May or October if you can – the crowds at Easter and from June to September can be frustrating; spending Christmas in Venice is fashionable nowadays. In the winter the city can be dank and cold, but this does give it a rather mystical beauty.**

Rooftop views from the Campanile di San Marco

SAN MARCO

The first area in Venice that most visitors head for is San
Marco, home to several of the city's main landmarks, notably
the Basilica di San Marco. For many tourists – daytrippers
with time only to flit in and out of the city – this is the only
part of Venice that they see. It's certainly a good place to start.

Piazza San Marco

The main square in Venice, **Piazza San Marco**, is a hectic
spot, bustling with tour groups and with pigeons who will
descend on anyone who cares to feed them. The square was
originally the site of a monastery garden with a canal running through it, but since its transformation in the 12th and
13th centuries it has been the religious and political centre of
the city. The Piazza has always pulled in the crowds – at the
peak of the Republic's powers, some of the world's most
spectacular processions, such as the one depicted in Bellini's

celebrated painting at the Accademia *(see page 51)*, were staged here. Victorious commanders returning home from the Genoese or Turkish wars were fêted in front of the Basilica with grand parades, while vendors on the square sold sweets and snacks, much as they do today. And under the arcades, Venetians and tourists have promenaded and been enchanted by elegant shops for centuries.

Yet despite all its pomp and circumstance and hustle and bustle, the Piazza remains a very civilised place. Dubbed by Napoleon the 'finest drawing room in Europe', it is elegantly proportioned, with colonnades on three sides, fringed with exquisite monuments (most dating from the 16th and 17th centuries) and completely free of traffic. Interestingly, the 'square' is actually a trapezoid, with uneven pavements sloping slightly downwards towards the Basilica. Its trachyte (volcanic rock) paving strips are more than 250 years old and lie over five or six earlier layers of tiles from the mid-13th century.

Campanile di San Marco

For the most breathtaking views of the Piazza and the city, take a lift to ascend the 100m (335ft) of Venice's tallest building, the **Campanile di San Marco** (St Mark's Belltower; open Apr–June, Sept–Oct daily 9am–7pm; July–Aug 9am–9pm; Nov–Mar 9.30am–4.15pm; admission fee), which over the years has served as a lighthouse, gun turret and belfry. Within less than a minute, the exotic domes of the Basilica, the splendid wedge-shaped tip of the Dorsoduro (marking

Close-up of the Campanile

the start of the Grand Canal) and the island church of San Giorgio Maggiore all lie beneath your feet, while all around are the terracotta-coloured tiles of the ancient city roofscape. The scene looks much the same now as it did over 200 years ago when the German writer J.W. von Goethe came here for his first view of the sea. It may well even look the same as it did four centuries ago when, according to local lore, Galileo brought the doge up here to show off his new telescope. Intriguingly, not a single canal can be seen from the Campanile.

However, this most potent symbol of the city is not the original tower, which collapsed into the Piazza on 14 July 1902. Fortunately, the old building creaked and groaned so much in advance that everyone knew what was coming – numerous belltowers in Venice have fallen down over the centuries, so the locals were used to it and knew to keep their distance; the eventual collapse caused no injury. Contrary to the 'evidence' supplied on cleverly faked postcards on sale throughout the city, the moment was not caught on film.

Coffee on the Piazza

The city council quickly decided to rebuild the bell tower 'as it was, where it was', and precisely 1,000 years after the erection of the original Campanile, on 25 April 1912 the new, lighter version was inaugurated. Fans of Venice around the world, many of whom had contributed funds to the project, were delighted. However, like many Venetian belltowers, this one is already starting to lean.

Piazza façade

Torre dell'Orologio

The Campanile is not the Piazza's only notable belltower – the graceful **Torre dell'Orologio** (Clock Tower; currently closed for restoration), featuring a splendid **zodiacal clock** that shows the time in both Arabic and Roman numerals, has been ticking for over 500 years. On Epiphany in January and through Ascension week in May three bright-eyed Magi and a trumpeting angel swing out from the face of the clock tower on the stroke of every hour and, stiffly bowing, ceremoniously rotate around a gilded Madonna.

At the top of the tower, two scantily clad North African bronze figures use hammers to strike a bell. According to Venetian legend, stroking the figures' exposed nether regions confers sexual potency for a year. Venetians also claim that a workman was knocked off the top of the tower in the 19th century by one of the hammers – perhaps a kind of revenge for the impertinence that the statues constantly have to endure.

Procuratie Vecchie and Nuove

Adjacent to the Torre dell'Orologio is the colonnaded **Procuratie Vecchie**, built in the 16th century as home to the Procurators of San Marco (state officers charged with the administration of the *sestieri*, or Venetian districts). Below it is

> In Venice's churches, especially the Basilica di San Marco, visitors in short shorts and vests will not be allowed entry. Shoulders and backs must be covered.

one of Venice's two most famous cafés, the Caffè Quadri, favoured haunt of the Austrians during their occupation of the city in the 19th century.

The church of **San Geminiamo** once stood at the far end of the Piazza opposite the Basilica, but in 1807 Napoleon ordered it to be demolished in order to make way for a wing joining the two sides of the square. On the façade of this wing, known as the **Ala Napoleonica** (Napoleon's Wing), there are several statues of Roman emperors and a central niche originally intended for a statue of Napoleon himself but pointedly left empty.

Opposite the Procuratie Vecchie is the **Procuratie Nuove**, built between 1582 and 1640 as a new home for the Procurators, and later occupied by Napoleon as a royal palace. The Museo Correr (see page 40) now occupies most of the upper floors of this building and the adjacent Ala Napoleonica. Below the Procuratie Nuove, on the side of the square facing Caffè Quadri, is the Piazza's other famous café, Florian. Founded in 1720, but with a mid-19th-century interior, it may be the oldest continuously operating café in the world.

Piazzetta dei Leoncini

The small square situated to the left as you face the Basilica is known as the **Piazzetta dei Leoncini**, after the two marble lions that have been here since 1722. On the side of the Basilica facing the Piazzetta is the tomb of Daniele Manin, the leader of Venice's revolt against Austria and the subsequent, short-lived Venetian Republic of 1848–9. A descendent of a family from the Venetian Ghetto, the heroic Manin was reinterred in this site of unequalled honour after the end of the

Austrian Occupation in 1866, along with his wife and children – none of the doges was granted such a splendid resting place.

Basilica di San Marco

Blending Eastern and Western elements, the **Basilica di** ◀
San Marco (St Mark's Basilica; open Mon–Sat May–Sept 9.45am–5.30pm; Oct–Apr until 4.30pm; Sun and hols 2–4pm; leave bags in the Ateneo San Basso, Calle San Basso 315/A open Mon–Fri 10am–4pm, holidays 2–4pm) is an exquisite, sumptuous shrine, encapsulating the old Republic's vision of itself as the successor to Constantinople. Despite the sloping irregular floors, an eclectic mix of styles both inside and out, the five low domes of totally unequal proportions and some 500 non-matching columns, San Marco still manages to convey a sense of grandeur as well as a jewel-like delicacy.

Basilica di San Marco

Mosaic in the narthex

The church was originally built in AD830 as a chapel for the doges and as a resting place for the remains of St Mark, then recently stolen from Alexandria by two Venetian adventurers *(see page 13)*. According to legend, they hid the body in a consignment of salted pork; Muslim customs officials, forbidden by their religion from eating or coming in contact with pork, did not do a thorough search and let the relics slip through their fingers. Not only were the body and many of the adornments in the Basilica stolen from the East but most of the church's columns were also in fact brought back as booty from forays into the Levant. The Basilica became the Republic's shrine as well as the coronation place of its doges. However, in 976, the original, largely wooden church burned down, and the Basilica we see today was constructed between 1063 and 1094; its exterior was then lavishly decorated with marble and ornamentation over the next three centuries.

The Narthex

The small porch at the entrance to the cathedral (the narthex) is a good place to first experience the fabulous **mosaics** that are a predominant feature of the church's interior (in total, they are said to cover around 0.5 hectares/1 acre) and were described by the poet W.B. Yeats as 'God's holy fire'. The narthex mosaics date from the 13th century and are among the most spectacular in the whole Basilica; they depict such Old Testament events as the Creation and the story of Noah's ark. See the mosaics in all their glory from 11.30am–12.30pm daily, and on Saturday afternoons, when the cathedral is illuminated.

Museo Marciano

The staircase immediately to the right of the main entrance leads to a small museum, the **Museo Marciano** (admission fee), housing some of the San Marco's finest treasures. The star attraction is the world's only surviving ancient *quadriga* (four horses abreast), known as the **Cavalli di San Marco** (The Horses of St Mark) and cast around AD200, either in Rome or Greece. At one time, the horses were believed to have crowned Trajan's Arch in Rome, but they were later moved to the imperial hippodrome in Constantinople, where Doge Dandolo claimed them as spoils of war in 1204, bringing them back to Venice. After guarding the shipyard of the

The Cavalli di San Marco, stolen from Constantinople

Venetian Arsenale for a while, the *quadriga* was moved to the front of the cathedral, becoming almost as symbolic of the city as St Mark's trademark lion.

In 1378 the rival republic of Genoa boasted that it would 'bridle those unbridled horses', but it never succeeded. Napoleon managed to corral them, however, taking them to Paris to stand on the Place du Carrousel adjacent to the Louvre for 13 years. When Venice fell under Austrian rule, the Austrians restored the horses to San Marco, where they remained until World War I, when the Italian government moved them to Rome. During World War II they were moved again, this time into the nearby countryside. After the war, they were returned to the Basilica, although the ones on display at the front of the cathedral are only replicas – the original *quadriga* was moved inside to protect it against corrosion from air pollution. The Venetians have vowed that the

Detail of the Pala d'Oro

horses will never be allowed to leave their city again.

The galleries in which the museums are situated provide good views of the interior; while outside on the Loggia dei Cavalli you can look down on Piazza San Marco and the adjacent piazzetta.

Intricate dome mosaic

The Treasury and High Altar

Located just off the baptistry on the Basilica's right-hand side is the **Tesoro** (Treasury; admission fee), where you can see further riches looted from Constantinople at the time of the Fourth Crusade (1204). Close by is the **Altare Maggiore** (High Altar), which bears a *ciborium* (canopy) mounted on four alabaster columns dating from the seventh or eighth century; sculpted scenes from the lives of Christ and the Virgin Mary adorn the altar. In the illuminated grating is a sarcophagus containing the relics of St Mark.

The Pala d'Oro

Behind the altar is one of Christendom's greatest treasures, the **Pala d'Oro** (admission fee), a gold, bejewelled altar screen featuring dozens of scenes from the *Bible*. Originally crafted in the 12th century, the screen was embellished and enlarged on the doges' orders until it reached its present stage in the mid-14th century. Its exquisitely wrought golden frame holds the Venetian equivalent of the Crown Jewels: 1,300 pearls, 400 garnets, 300 sapphires, 300 emeralds, 90 amethysts, 75 balas-rubies, 15 rubies, four topazes and two cameos.

The only drawback to the fabulous splendour of the Pala d'Oro is that it pulls in hordes of sightseers. The best way to try and beat the crowds is to visit either early in the morning, before day-trippers and tour groups have arrived, or late in the afternoon, after they have left.

Palazzo Ducale

For nine centuries the magnificent **Palazzo Ducale** ◄ (Doge's Palace; open Apr–Oct daily 9am–7pm; Nov–Mar 9am–5pm, last entrance one hour before closing time; admission fee) was the seat of the Republic, serving as a council chamber, law court and prison, as well as the residence of most of Venice's doges. The Palazzo was first built in fortress-like Byzantine style in the 9th century and partially replaced 500 years later by a Gothic structure. The architects of this massive structure, with peach-and-white patternings in its brick façade, achieved an incredible delicacy by balancing the bulk of the building above two floors of Gothic arcades. The ravages inflicted by three devastating fires have meant some extensive reconstruction work has been carried out on the building over the centuries.

The palace's 15th-century ceremonial entrance, the **Porta della Carta** (Paper Gate), is a masterpiece of late Gothic stonework. Its name may derive from the fact that the doge's decrees were affixed here, or from the professional scribes who

Venetian Doge

set up nearby. On the left, note the four curious dark brown figures of the Tetrarchs (also known as the 'Four Moors'), variously said to represent the Roman emperor Diocletian and associates, or four Saracen robbers who tried to loot the Basilica's Treasury *(see page 33)* through the wall behind them.

Visits start at the Porta del Frumento on the lagoon side of the palace. The **Museo dell' Opera** by the entrance houses some of the original carved capitals from the palazzo's loggias. Inside the courtyard is the impressive ceremonial stairway, the **Scala dei Giganti**, named after Sansovino's colossal statues of Neptune and Mars (symbolising, respectively, Venetian sea and land powers). Visitors use the only slightly less grandiose **Scala d'Oro** (Golden Staircase), which was built during the 16th century to designs by Jacopo Sansovino.

The Interior

The former private quarters of the doges are occasionally sectioned off from the rest of the palace and used for temporary exhibitions. Although mostly unfurnished, these rooms still retain their finely decorated ceilings, magnificent fireplaces and the occasional grand painting.

The main tour of the palace begins in the state rooms, in which the business of the *Serenissima* was once conducted. This part of the complex is home to some of the finest paintings in the ducal collection. On the walls in front of and behind you as you enter the **Anticollegio** are four allegories by Tintoretto, combining images of

Columns from the interior of the Palazzo Ducale

pagan gods and the four seasons to suggest that Venice is favoured at all times. Jacob Bassano's *Jacob Returning to Canaan* is on the wall opposite the windows, on your right. To the left of it is Veronese's masterpiece, *The Rape of Europa*.

Proceed on to the **Sala del Collegio**, where the doges received ambassadors. Next is the **Sala del Senato** where the Venetian ruling council (made up of the doge, his advisors, members of the judiciary and senators) formulated policy.

The next room is the **Sala del Consiglio dei Dieci**, the meeting room of the Council of Ten. The Ten (who actually numbered up to 17) formed a high-ranking group that met on matters of state security and acquired a reputation similar to that of the secret police. A letter-box in the form of a lion's mouth, for the use of citizens who wished to inform the Ten of anything untoward, can be seen in the next room. A door in the corner of this room leads to the prisons. This route can only be taken as part of a special tour (in English, French and Italian, daily at 9.55am, 10.45am and 11.35 in English; tel: 041-520 90 70 preferably 2 days in advance or ask at the Doge's Palace information desk, tel: 041-271 5911). The tour, which is known as the *Itinerari Segreti* (Secret Routes), includes the torture chamber (in reality far less gruesome than it sounds) and the cell from which Casanova, one of Venice's most notorious citizens, escaped in 1775.

Veronese's *Battle of Lepanto*

On the public route, the palace's somewhat menacing aura is confirmed by a splendid private armoury, in which some exceedingly gruesome weapons are displayed.

Palace façade

The route then leads down to the first-floor state rooms. The most resplendent of all, is the **Sala del Maggior Consiglio** (Great Council Chamber), a vast hall where Venetian citizens assembled to elect doges and debate state policies in the early days of the Republic. Later, only the nobles convened here. The hall was built to hold an assembly of up to 1,700, but by the mid-16th century this figure had increased to around 2,500.

Covering the whole of one end wall is Tintoretto's *Paradiso*, based on Dante's masterpiece, and undertaken by the artist (with the assistance of his son) while he was in his seventies. At 7m by 22m (23ft by 72ft), it is the largest old master oil painting in the world, containing some 350 human figures. Adorning the ceiling is Veronese's *Apotheosis of Venice*, which captures the ideal civic conception of Venice as serene, prosperous, elegant and self-assured. Portraits of 76 doges (several of which are little more than artistic guesswork) line the cornice beneath the ceiling. Conspicuously absent is the 14th-century doge, Marin Falier – a black veil marks his intended place of honour, and a notice tells us that he was beheaded for treason in 1355. From here the tour takes you to the criminal courts and the **Prigioni Nuove** (New Prisons), reached by the Bridge of Sighs (*see box below*). Visits end at the offices of the Avogaria (court clerks).

Piazzetta San Marco

If Piazza San Marco is the drawing room of Venice, then the smaller Piazzetta San Marco is its vestibule. The two soaring **granite columns** dominating the *piazzetta* were stolen from the East and hoisted upright here in 1172. They haven't moved since, although a third column apparently fell into the sea, never to be recovered.

On top of one of the columns is Venice's original patron saint, St Theodore; on the other stands what must be the strangest looking of the city's many stone lions – not really a lion at all but a *chimera*, a mythical hybrid beast (you

---

Bridge of Sighs

Pass through narrow corridors of the Palazzo Ducale and across the legendary **Ponte dei Sospiri** (Bridge of Sighs), built in 1603, and recall the lines written by Lord Byron, 'I stood in Venice on the Bridge of Sighs, a palace and a prison on each hand.' As you will discover when recrossing this baroque stone bridge, it has two parallel passageways, presumably so that prisoners on their way to the Council of Ten would not meet those who had already been interrogated. The name seems to derive more from romantic fiction than hard fact, as only petty criminals would have made this journey. You can see the small, dark cells in which they were kept, but don't expect grisly instruments of torture; by medieval standards, these dungeons were relatively civilised.

can see it most clearly from the balcony of the Palazzo Ducale). Even though its exact origin is unknown, it is thought to be of Eastern provenance and may be up to 2,200 years old.

Nowadays, the area between the columns bustles with tourists, but between the 15th and mid-18th centuries this was a place of execution. One of the more creative punishments for treason involved torturing the prisoner, burning them on a raft, dragging them through the streets by a horse and finally putting them to death between the columns.

The Bridge of Sighs

The Biblioteca Nazionale Marciana and Gardinetti Reali

The lavish 16th-century building opposite the Palazzo Ducale has its own café and orchestra but is in fact a library. This is the **Biblioteca Nazionale Marciana** (combined ticket and access via Museo Correr, *see page 40*), also known as the Libreria **Sansoviniana** after its architect Jacopo Sansovino. You can take a peek inside the porch, which is dominated by two giant statues. The building also houses the Museo Archeologico *(see page 41)*.

Just a few yards behind the library are the **Giardinetti Reali** (Royal Gardens). There are tourist information offices *(see page 126)* close by in Palazzetto Selva, and at the southwest exit of Piazza San Marco, opposite the Basilica.

Museums of the Piazza

There are two museums on Piazza San Marco, both of which are usually not too crowded. The **Museo Correr** (same hours as Palazzo Ducale, *see page 34*, and joint ticket), visited on a combined ticket with the other St Mark's museums) is home to the city museum and contains artefacts from virtually every aspect of Venice's history. It houses a fine collection of 14th- to 16th-century Venetian paintings, including a room of works by Jacopo Bellini and his sons, Giovanni and Gentile. Vittorie Carpaccio's *Two Venetian Noblewomen*, traditionally and erroneously known as *The Courtesans*, is also displayed here.

Other highlights of the Museo Correr include sculpture by Canova, naval sections with wonderful globes of the old world and items of clothing such as incredible stilt-like platform shoes worn by 15th-century Venetian courtesans. Within the Correr is the **Museo del Risorgimento**,

Negotiating the city's unusual geography

which illustrates the history of Venice from the 19th century onwards.

Venice's **Museo Archeologico** (Archaeological Museum; access through Museo Correr, same opening hours and joint ticket) is also on the Piazza. The core collection consists of Greek and Roman sculpture bequeathed by Cardinal Grimani in 1523, a gift that influenced generations of Venetian artists who came to study here. Among the Roman busts, medals, coins, cameos and portraits are Greek originals and Roman copies, including a 5th-century Hellenistic *Persephone*.

The Scala del Bovolo

Also in the Area

If you have more time to explore this area, there is a rather intriguing tower and three further churches, all within a few minutes' walk of Piazza San Marco.

Scala del Bovolo

Hidden in a maze of alleys between Calle Vida and Calle Contarini, not far from Campo Manin (*campo* = square), is **Palazzo Contarini del Bovolo** (open daily 10am–6pm, until 4pm off season; admission fee), a late-Gothic palace renowned for its lovely romantic arcaded staircase, the **Scala del Bovolo**. *Bovolo* means 'snail-shell' in Venetian dialect and fittingly describes this graceful spiral staircase, which is linked to loggias of brick and smooth white stone. The palace is now open to the public, but you don't need access to see the stairway.

San Zaccaria

A mere three minutes' walk east of Piazza San Marco is the splendid early 16th-century church of **San Zaccaria** (open daily 10am–noon and 4–6pm). Supposedly the last resting place of Zaccharias (the father of John the Baptist), whose body lies in the right aisle, this Gothic-Renaissance masterpiece features Giovanni Bellini's celebrated *Madonna and Child*. In the side chapels are splendid glowing altarpieces, and the eerie, permanently flooded 8th-century crypt, where several early doges rest in watery graves, is one of the most atmospheric spots in the city.

Santo Stefano and Santa Maria Formosa

In contrast to the seldom-visited spots just listed, the churches of Santo Stefano and Santa Maria Formosa are situated on two of the area's busiest squares. The Gothic

Bellini's *Madonna and Child*

Santo Stefano (open Mon–
Sat 10am–5pm, Sun 1–5pm;
admission fee), located on
Campo Santo Stefano, west
of Piazza San Marco, is a
large, airy structure decorated with rich ornamen-
tation and works by
Tintoretto. The church is a
favourite Venetian concert
venue. On the lively
**Campo Santa Maria For-
mosa**, a short walk north-
west of Piazza San Marco,
is the 15th-century church
of the same name (same

San Giorgio degli Schiavoni

hours as above; admission fee), which is noted for its altar-
piece by Palma il Vecchio.

Scuola di San Giorgio degli Schiavoni

In the San Zaccaria neighbourhood, not far from San Marco,
is the **Scuola di San Giorgio degli Schiavoni** (open Apr–
Oct Tues–Sat 9.30am–12.30pm, 3.30–6.30pm, Sun 9.30am–
12.30pm; Nov–Mar Tues–Sat 10am–12.30pm, 3–6pm, Sun
10am–12.30pm; admission fee). The five Venetian *scuole*
were craft guilds of laymen under the banner of a particular
saint, and this one was founded in 1451 as the guildhall of
the city's Dalmatian merchants. In the early 16th century
these Slavs *(Schiavoni)*, prospering from trade with the East,
commissioned Vittorio Carpaccio to decorate their hall. His
nine pictures, completed between 1502 and 1508, decorate
the lower floor and depict the lives of the three Dalmatian
patron saints: Jerome, Tryphone and George. Note Carpaccio's gory *St George and the Dragon.*

ALONG THE WATERFRONT

There are few more stately waterfronts in the world than that of Venice's splendid *riva* (quay), which curves gently away from San Marco and enters the *sestiere* (district) of Castello.

The Riva degli Schiavoni

The first section, the **Riva degli Schiavoni** (Quay of the Slavs), begins in front of the Palazzo Ducale *(see page 34)*. The quay takes its name from the Dalmatian merchants who used to tie up their boats here – vessels laden with wares from the East. This is still a place of trade, though less exotic

Gondolas moored along the quay

than in its heyday, with souvenir stalls and ice-cream and refreshment stands lining the banks. Boats still moor here, too: *vaporetti* (waterbuses) at the busy station of San Zaccaria and fleets of gondolas waiting to tempt tourists.

After the Palazzo Ducale, the next sight you'll see (with your back to the waterfront) is the Bridge of Sighs *(see page 38)*. A little further on is the red **Palazzo Dandolo**, now the legendary **Hotel Danieli**, with a lavish neo-Gothic lobby that's worth a look. When Proust stayed here, he declared, 'When I went to Venice I found that my dream had become – incredibly but quite simply – my address'. The Danieli was also the scene of an unhappy love affair between the writers George Sand and Alfred de Musset in 1883.

Beyond is the church of **La Pietà** (open daily 9.30am–noon), a handsome building with a fine ceiling painting by Giambattista Tiepolo. It is known as 'Vivaldi's church', after Antonio Vivaldi who was concertmaster here from 1705 to 1740.

Carry on past the statue of King Vittorio Emanuele II and you'll notice the crowds starting to thin out. By the time you reach the Arsenale *vaporetto* stop, just a short stretch from the Palazzo Ducale, the crowds will probably have dispersed completely, even in high season.

The Arsenale

For 700 years, before Napoleon's invasion in the late 18th century, the Republic's galleys and galleons were built at the **Arsenale** (closed to the public), once the greatest shipyard in the world. Dante visited it, and used the images of its workers, toiling amid cauldrons of boiling pitch, as the inspiration for his *Inferno*. *Arsenale*, originally from the Arabic for 'house of industry', is one of those Venetian coinages that have passed into universal usage. The yard also originated the concept of the assembly line. Output was prodigious.

One of the yard's proudest achievements came in 1574, while Henri III of France was visiting Venice. In the time it took for the French king to get through his state banquet at the Palazzo Ducale, the workers at the Arsenale had constructed a fully equipped galley from scratch, ready for the king's inspection.

Today, there's little to remind visitors of those heady days. Napoleon destroyed the Arsenale in 1797, and al-

---

The Lions of Venice

Pacific, playful or warlike, lions dominate paintings, sculptures, crests and illuminated manuscripts in Venice; they adorn buildings, bridges, balconies, archways and doorways, with the greatest concentration in the San Marco and Castello districts, closest to the centre of power. Whereas the seated lion represents the majesty of state, the walking lion symbolises Venetian sovereignty over its dominions. The Lion of St Mark bears a traditional greeting of peace and in times of war is depicted with a closed book, as in the arch over the Arsenale gateway. A few lions are shown clutching a drawn sword in one of their paws. The Napoleonic forces were well aware of the symbolism of lions and destroyed many prominent images; as a result, some, such as those on the Gothic gateway to the Palazzo Ducale, are replicas.

though it was rebuilt by the Austrians, operations here ceased in 1917. The shipyard is now mainly used by the navy, although some of the buildings serve as exhibition space during La Biennale *(see page 89)* and as a venue for the occasional theatre or concert. At the entrance visitors can only admire the impressive 15th-century gateway, guarded by a motley collection of white stone lions, all stolen from ancient Greek sites.

Lion on the gate of the Arsenale

The two on the river side are believed to date back to the 6th century BC.

Museo Storico Navale

The nearest you will get to the spirit of the age is in the **Museo Storico Navale** (Naval History Museum; open Mon–Fri 8.45am–1.30pm, Sat morning only; admission fee). For many visitors the star attraction is the model of the last *Bucintoro*, the gilded barge that was used by the doge on state occasions, although entire sections of other state barges and warships are also on show. Don't miss the atmospheric annexe – displaying a range of ships – housed in the old **naval sheds** close to the Arsenale entrance, on the right-hand side of the river.

Unless you're heading for the Biennale exhibition *(see page 89)* there's little of sightseeing interest further east along the waterfront. It's worth coming this far, however, simply for the splendid views back towards the Palazzo Ducale.

The Fondamenta Venier in the Dorsoduro

DORSODURO

'Dorsoduro' is a name with which few first-time visitors to Venice will be familiar, yet most will visit this *sestiere* to see the city's main art gallery, the Accademia, or the iconic Santa Maria della Salute church. Dorsoduro encompasses the section of Venice that lies just across the Grand Canal from San Marco. Its eastern boundary is marked by the Punta della Dogana; its northern one by the Rio Nuovo–Rio Foscari.

Dorsoduro is perhaps the most picturesque part of Venice. Within this quiet residential area are three of the city's finest art collections, numerous excellent restaurants and shops, and the city's university.

The Accademia

The **Galleria dell'Accademia** (Accademia Gallery; open Mon 8.15am–2pm, Tues–Sun until 7.15pm; admission fee) is home to the most pre-eminent collection of Venetian art in existence and is the most-visited spot in the city after Piazza San Marco and the Palazzo Ducale. A maximum of 180 visitors are allowed in at any one time, so arrive early to avoid the queues.

The collection spans paintings from the 14th to the 18th centuries, arranged roughly chronologically in 24 rooms. Visitors with only a limited amount of time to spare can hardly expect to absorb all the riches displayed here, and it's sensible to be selective rather than try and see everything and take in nothing. The following summary of the museum's highlights should help you make the most of your visit.

Room 2 contains Carpaccio's striking *Crucifixion of the Ten Thousand Martyrs*, while **Room 4** draws crowds of art lovers for its exquisite group of paintings, including Mantegna's *St George* and a fine series of works by Giovanni Bellini and Giorgione. **Room 5** holds the most famous work of art in the gallery, Giorgione's *Tempest*, a moody and enigmatic canvas; it also houses *Portrait of an Old Woman,* by the same artist.

In **Room 10** look out for Veronese's *Feast at the House of Levi*, a painting of a raucous Renaissance banquet originally entitled (and meant to depict) the *Last Supper.* When church officials condemned the work as sacrilegious and ordered Veronese to change it, he blithely did nothing but change its name. Jacopo Tintoretto's dazzling St Mark paintings, notably the haunting *Transport of the Body of St Mark*, are also

Tintoretto's *Transport of St Mark*, Accademia collection

here, as is Titian's dark *Pietà*, the artist's last work, intended for his tomb. **Room 11** contains masterpieces by Veronese and Tintoretto, as well as Tiepolo's *Rape of Europa*, a triumph of pulsating light and shade, while **Room 17** contains a real Venetian rarity – a painting by Canaletto; this is the Accademia's only work by this artist.

Out of sequence, **Room 23** is housed in the top of the church that constitutes part of the gallery structure. The airy, spacious

Venetian Artists

- **Jacopo Bellini** (1400–70) and his sons **Giovanni** (1430–1516) and **Gentile** (1429–1507) inaugurated the *Serenissima's* glorious era of art in the 15th century.
- The Venetian High Renaissance began with **Giorgione** (c.1477–1510), whose great promise can be seen in *Tempest*, at the Accademia.
- **Vittore Carpaccio** (1445–1526) painted detailed scenes of city life as well as the splendid series on the life of St Ursula at the Accademia.
- **Titian** (1490–1576) was widely hailed as the finest painter of his era. Only a few of his works can be seen in Venice; these include the *Assumption of the Virgin*, above the altar of the Frari church.
- **Jacopo Tintoretto** (1518–94) was a quiet, religious man who left Venice only once. Most of his work remains in the city. See his genius in the Scuola di San Rocco and his parish church of Madonna dell'Orto.
- **Paolo Veronese** (1528–88) is inextricably linked with the church of San Sebastiano, which is resplendent with his paintings. Many of his works are in the Accademia.
- **Antonio Canaletto** (1697–1768) is famed for his detailed paintings of Venice but only three are on show in the city – most were sold abroad by his English patron, Josef Smith.
- Perhaps the greatest Venetian decorative painter was **Giovanni Battista Tiepolo** (1696–1770), who covered the ceiling of the upper hall in the Scuola Grande dei Carmini with nine masterly paintings.

loft is the perfect setting for some splendid altarpieces, notably the faded but powerful *Blessed Lorenzo Giustinian* by Gentile Bellini. **Room 20** is probably the most stunning in the Accademia, with four immense paintings occupying one wall apiece. Gentile Bellini's celebrated *Procession Around the Piazza Bearing the Cross* reveals how little San Marco has changed since 1496, except for its mosaics and the addition of the Campanile and Procuratie Nuove. Other il-

Detail from Carpaccio's St Ursula cycle, Accademia collection

lustrious paintings include Carpaccio's epic *Miracle of the Holy Cross at the Rialto Bridge*, showing the old bridge at the Rialto *(see page 58)* and gondolas on the Grand Canal.

In **Room 21** is Carpaccio's lyrical, poetically narrative *St Ursula* cycle, which depicts the tragic life of this Breton heroine. It spans her acceptance of the hand of the British prince, Hereus, on condition of his conversion to Christianity, to their subsequent pilgrimage to Rome and eventual martyrdom at the hands of Attila the Hun.

The top floor has been opened to house works from the permanent collections as well as temporary exhibitions and travelling shows.

Collezione Peggy Guggenheim

Just to the east of the Accademia along the Grand Canal, in the Palazzo Venier dei Leoni *(see also page 70)*, is another exceptional museum, the **Collezione Peggy Guggenheim**

Henry Moore sculpture at the Collezione Peggy Guggenheim

(open Wed–Mon 10am–6pm, open later in summer; admission fee), which is generally regarded as one of the best and most comprehensive collections of modern art in Europe. The bequest of American expatriate and heiress Peggy Guggenheim, who died in 1979, is displayed in the building she made her home: an eccentrically designed, one-storey 18th-century palace (still unfinished), with its gardens and terrace overlooking the Grand Canal. Guggenheim was renowned for her hospitality, and the administrators of the Collezione have tried to make the museum especially welcoming. The museum café, with a menu designed by the owner of Ai Gondolieri, is one of the better restaurants in Venice.

Among the outstanding exhibits are early Picassos and Chagalls and Brancusi's bronze sculpture *Bird in Space*. Other highlights include works by Max Ernst (whom Guggenheim married), Dalí, Miró, Piet Mondrian and Jackson Pollock, as well as a sculpture by Calder that Guggenheim used in lieu of a headboard for her bed. Sculptures by Giacometti dot the garden. Don't miss Marino Marini's *Angel of the Citadel*, a bold, joyfully erotic bronze equestrian statue in the garden facing the Grand Canal.

For more modern art, try the waterfront **Galleria Cini** (open only for special exhibitions; <www.cini.it>) at Piscina del Forner 864, between the Guggenheim and the Accademia.

La Salute

Having presided over the entrance to the Grand Canal for over 300 years, the magnificent baroque church of **Santa Maria della Salute** (open daily 9am–5.30pm) is almost as familiar a Venetian landmark as the Basilica di San Marco.

The church, popularly known among the Venetians as **La Salute**, was built as an offering of thanks to the Virgin Mary for the end of a catastrophic plague in 1630 – the plague wiped out over a third of the lagoon's inhabitants. Under the direction of the young architect, Baldassare Longhena, construction began in 1631, and more than one million oak pilings were sunk into the swampy earth to support the massive structure. Longhena lived to see the church, his life's work, completed in 1682. Each year, on 21 November, the church's feast day (Festa della Salute), engineers build a great pontoon of boats over the Grand Canal, and most of the city's population, resident and visiting, join a procession across the water and into the church. This is the only day that the church's main doors are opened.

Il Redentore *(see page 55)*

Inside, in the sacristy to the left of the high altar, is Tintoretto's magnificent painting of the *Marriage at Cana*. Three Titians (*Cain and Abel*, *Abraham Sacrificing Isaac* and *David and Goliath*) are also on view.

The Dogana and Zattere

Continue east from the Salute towards the tip of Dorsoduro. At this point (restoration work permitting), you'll find the 17th-century **Dogana di Mare** (Customs House), where the cargos from all incoming ships were inspected in former days. Atop the tower of the Dogana is the curious balletic wind-vane showing the figure of Fortune (also possibly representing justice), holding a ship's rudder and set on a large gilded globe supported by two Atlas-like figures.

Traditional gondolier's garb

The views from here, looking straight into the Bacino di San Marco (St Mark's Basin) in one direction and across the **Canale della Giudecca** (Giudecca Canal) in the other, are among the most breathtaking in the whole city. This is the beginning of the Fondamente delle Zattere (Quay of the Rafts), a long stretch that runs along the waterfront all the way to the Rio di San Sebastiano. The floating rafts that gave the Zattere its name were once major unloading points for cargoes of salt and other such valuable commodities. The huge salt warehouse, once capable of storing over 40,000 tons of the mineral, is now partly used as a boathouse for a local rowing club.

From the Punta della Dogana look out across the Canale della Giudecca to the islands of Giudecca and San Giorgio

Maggiore; this vista takes in three churches designed by Andrea Palladio: the imposing church of **San Giorgio Maggiore** *(see page 76)*, **Le Zitelle** (the Church of the Spinsters) and the grand church of the **Redentore** (Redeemer, *see picture on page 53)*. The last was built, like the Salute after it, as an act of thanksgiving at the end of the devastating plague of 1575–6. As at the Salute, there is an annual celebration at the Redentore each third Sunday of July; the festivities culminate in a flotilla of small boats and a spectacular display of fireworks over the water.

Continue along the Zattere past the churches of Spirito Santo and the Gesuati (Santa Maria del Rosario). Turn right on to the Fondamenta Nani and a few yards further along on the opposite side you will see the rustic **Squero di San**

Gondolas and Gondoliers

Nothing is more quintessentially Venetian than the gondola, although nowadays they are more a tourist attraction than a means of transportation. Gondolas have existed since the 11th century, and in the 18th century around 14,000 plied Venice's canals; today, the number has fallen to 400. All gondolas are made to the same specifications, built by hand from around 280 separate pieces of wood. Curiously, they are asymmetrical (the left side is wider than the right) in order to accommodate the gondolier as he rows and steers. Gondolas are painted black in deference to the sumptuary laws of 1562 that attempted to curb the extravagances of Venetian society. They also retain a rather curious metallic pronged prow (or *ferro*). Several explanations have been offered for the symbolism and shape of the *ferro*: some think that the blades represent the six districts of Venice; others maintain that the shape suggests the Grand Canal or even the doge's cap. Many gondoliers still wear the traditional outfit of straw boater, striped T-shirt and white sailor's top, although these days, if you want to be serenaded, that will cost extra.

Venetian backwater

Trovaso (*squero* means boat-yard). In the 16th century, when thousands of gondolas plied the waters of Venice, there were many *squeri*; nowadays, just four remain in operation, and San Trovaso is the only one where you can see gondolas and other craft waiting to be repaired. The church of **San Trovaso** (open Mon–Sat 3–5pm) is worth investigating for two of Tintoretto's last works, both completed by his son.

Head back to the Zattere, which, with its cafés and restaurants, is a good place to take a break. The huge red-brick landmark that you can see across the water right at the western end of Giudecca is the **Mulino Stucky** (Stucky's Mill), a flour mill that was part of an attempt to bring modern industry to Venice in the 1890s. It closed in 1954 and remained deserted until the late 1990s; it will soon reopen as a hotel and conference centre.

The University Quarter

The attractive area between the Accademia and Campo Santa Margherita, is pervaded (but not dominated) by the city's University. At Campo San Barnaba you'll see an attractive fruit-and-vegetable barge moored along the quay, and the solemn, Neo-Classical church of San Barnaba, which film buffs may recognise as the setting for major scenes in *Sum-*

mertime (with Katharine Hepburn) and *Indiana Jones and the Last Crusade*. In term time **Campo Santa Margherita**, home to numerous inexpensive restaurants, bohemian shops and colourful market stalls, is the liveliest square in Venice outside Piazza San Marco. At one end of the square is the restored church of Santa Margherita, while at the other end is the spacious and ornately decorated **Chiesa dei Carmini** (Church of the Carmelites). For even more religious art, call in next door at **I Carmini** (open Apr–Oct daily 9am–6pm; Nov–Mar daily 9am–4pm; admission fee), the headquarters of the Scuola Grande dei Carmini and a showcase for the work of Tiepolo, who covered the ceiling of the Upper Hall with nine paintings, the last one completed in 1744.

SAN POLO AND SANTA CROCE

The two adjoining *sestieri* of San Polo and Santa Croce are curved into the left bank of the Grand Canal. Together they are home to many important sights, including the artistic treasure houses of the church of the Frari and the Scuola Grande di San Rocco, as well as one of the city's most vibrant attractions: the Rialto markets.

The Rialto

Not only the oldest district in Venice, the Rialto is also the area of the city with the greatest concentration of Veneto-Byzantine palaces. From its earliest foundation, this was the powerhouse of the Republic, and a crossroads between the East and the West. On a practical level, it also acted as a busy

Looking out from the Rialto

commercial exchange and meeting place for merchants. As such, the Rialto is often described as 'Venice's kitchen, office and back parlour'. During the peak of the Republic's influence it was one of the most important financial centres in Europe (reflected in Shakespeare's *Merchant of Venice*, when Shylock asks of Bassanio, 'What news on the Rialto?').

Ponte di Rialto

► The **Ponte di Rialto** (Rialto Bridge) traditionally divides the city into two, with the right bank, on the San Marco side, known as the *Rialto di quà* (this side), and the left bank known as the *Rialto di là* (that side). The bridge spans the Grand Canal with a strong, elegantly curved arch of marble, and is lined with shops selling silk ties, scarves, leather and jewellery. Henry James appreciated the 'small shops and booths that abound in Venetian character' but also felt 'the communication of insect life'.

The current bridge is merely the last in a line that began with simple pontoons and then progressed to a wooden structure, with a drawbridge section to allow the passage of tall ships. A new bridge was created in 1588–91 by Antonio da Ponte following the collapse of the previous one. Tradition has it that the greatest architects of the day, including Michelangelo and Palladio, competed for the commission, but the aptly named da Ponte was chosen. The result is a light, floating structure with shops nestling in its solid, closed arches. From the bridge one can admire the majestic sweep of palaces and warehouses swinging away to La Volta del Canal, the great elbow-like bend in the Grand Canal.

The Rialto Markets

► The other highlight of the Rialto is its **markets**, which make a refreshing change from the monumental Venice of San Marco. Ignore the tourist tat in favour of angora sweaters, leather shoes and foodstuffs galore, including pasta, cheese and salami. Ruga Vecchia di San Giovanni is home to some good food shops and close to several *bacari* (traditional Venetian wine bars).

The *Erberia* is a fruit-and-vegetable market overlooking the Grand Canal. Casanova spoke of it as a place for 'innocent pleasure', but latter-day foodies might find sensuous pleasure in the profusion of medicinal herbs, flowers, fruit and local vegetables – from asparagus and radicchio to baby artichokes – on offer here.

The markets extend along the bank to the *Pescheria,* the fish market, set in an arcaded neo-Gothic hall by the quayside, a design inspired by Carpaccio's realistic paintings. Under the porticos, fishermen set their catch on mountains of ice. The sight of so much appetising food is an invitation to a lively lunch in a local *bacaro*. The adjoining

Ponte di Rialto

Campo delle Beccarie, once a public abattoir, now contains market overspill and a lively bar.

Campo San Polo

The biggest *campo* (square) in the city outside Piazza San Marco, San Polo is notable for its church and for the mid-14th-century rose-coloured **Palazzo Soranzo**, situated just opposite. Casanova came to this palace in the 18th century as a young, hired violinist, living as the adopted son and heir to the family fortune with access to the very best of Venetian society. From here, he went on to seduce and outrage the world of Europe's 18th-century aristocracy.

Campo San Polo

Note the fine portal of the church of **San Polo** (open Mon–Sat 10am–5pm, Sun 1–5pm; admission fee), one of the few features that survives from the original 15th-century building. The interior, which is reached through a side door, features a brooding *Last Supper* by Tintoretto and Giandomenico Tiepolo's *Via Crucis (Stations of the Cross)* painted when he was only 20 years of age. A campanile, dating from 1362, stands a short way across from the church and is adorned with two of the Republic's less-appealing lions, one playing with a human head, the other with a serpent.

The Frari

> **Santa Maria Gloriosa dei Frari** (known simply as the Frari, a deformation of *frati*, meaning 'brothers'; open Mon–Sat 9am–6pm; Sun 1–6pm; admission fee) is Venice's second church after San Marco and the resting place of the painter Titian. The brothers in question – members of the Franciscan order – were granted a piece of land in 1236, and the church, a huge lofty structure, was rebuilt between 1340 and 1469.

Detail of Titian's *Assumption of the Virgin*, at the Frari

The church's greatest treasure is the soaring, mysterious *Assumption* (1518) hanging in the Gothic apse above the high altar. One of Titian's early masterpieces, this painting helped to establish his reputation. To the right is Donatello's much-admired wooden statue of *St John the Baptist*. Restored during the 19th century, it is the Florentine artist's sole remaining work in Venice. Also in this part of the church, tucked away in the sacristy, is the *Madonna and Saints* (1488), a triptych by Giovanni Bellini. Don't miss the beautiful marquetry and intricate carving on the choir stalls – this choir is one of the few in Venetian churches to stand in its original location.

The Frari is also notable for its huge monuments to Titian and to the 19th-century sculptor, Canova, on opposite sides of the great nave. Although Titian was buried here in 1576, the monument to him was not built until the mid-19th century. Canova's mausoleum was erected in 1827,

> **Before you leave the Frari church, be sure to note the splendid *Madonna di Ca' Pesaro* by Titian, which is thought to represent the artist's wife.**

five years after his death; however, only his heart is interred here.

Several doges are entombed in the Frari, including two in the high altar. The church is also home to one of the city's most bombastic monuments, which is dedicated to Doge Giovanni Pesaro and situated next to Canova's mausoleum.

Scuola Grande di San Rocco

➤ The **Scuola Grande di San Rocco** (open daily 9am–5.30pm, 4pm off season; admission fee) stirs the emotions. John Ruskin, the foremost Venetian art historian of the 19th century and one of the city's most scrupulous observers, described San Rocco as having one of the three most precious picture collections in all Italy (ranking it above the Accademia). The novelist Henry James was also a devotee, although he found the Scuola Grande a little too breathtaking, proclaiming it to be 'suffocating'.

San Rocco, formerly one of the five great Venetian *scuole* (*see page 43*), commissioned Tintoretto to decorate the interior, following the artist winning a competition in 1564 to take on the project. For the next 23 years much of the Tintoretto's time was spent painting the 65 pictures here.

Tintoretto begins upstairs in the sumptuous **Sala dell' Albergo**, just off the main hall, so make your way straight there before coming back down to the lower hall. His monumental *Crucifixion* (described by Ruskin as 'beyond all analysis and above all praise') is said to have been considered by the artist to be his greatest painting.

In the dimly lit main hall, the gilded **ceiling** is covered with 21 immense pictures, and there are another 13 on the walls (all of which are captioned on the helpful plan provided free at the entrance). The best way of studying the ceiling works is to focus on the detail, rather than attempting to take in broad sweeps at once. Hidden in the gloom below the murals are some wonderful, if slightly odd, wooden figures by Venice's off-beat 17th-century's sculptor Francesco Pianto.

In contrast to the pictures in the main hall, those on the ground floor (representing scenes from the life of the Virgin) seem almost playful. Look out for *The Flight into Egypt*, widely acknowledged as another of Tintoretto's great paintings. More Tin-
torettos are on display in the church of San Rocco next door.

Tintoretto's *Glory of St Roch*, Scuola Grande di San Rocco

Casa di Carlo Goldoni

Close to Campo San Polo and the Frari is the **Casa di Carlo Goldoni** (open Apr–Oct daily 10am–5pm; Nov–Mar daily 10am–4pm; admission fee), the house in which the playwright Carlo Goldoni was born in 1707. In 1952 the house was turned into a small museum dedicated to the writer and his works, and although the contents are quite specialist, the house is worth a visit for its well-preserved Gothic architecture, especially its handsome courtyard.

THE GRAND CANAL

The extraordinary main artery through Venice, the **Grand Canal** (Canal Grande) – or *Canalazzo*, as it is known to the locals – stretches over 4km (2 miles), from inauspicious beginnings near the Stazione Ferrovia (railway station) to a glorious final outpouring into the Basino di San Marco (St Mark's Basin). The views along the canal are so wonderful that many visitors ride the *vaporetti* back and forth for hours, soaking up the atmosphere; a good waterbus to take is the inappropriately named *accelerato* (No. 1), which stops at every landing stage.

The banks of the canal are lined with more than 200 ornate palaces and grand houses, mostly built between the 14th and 18th centuries. While some have been superbly restored, others have a neglected air, awaiting their turn for renovation. Very few of these homes are still inhabited by the aristocratic

Along the Grand Canal

families for whom they were built; the majority have been turned into offices, hotels, apartments or museum or gallery spaces.

The following section details some of the most outstanding palaces to look for while travelling along the canal from the railway station (Stazione Ferrovia) towards Piazza San Marco.

> **If you want to walk or dine alongside the canal, the place to do so is on the Riva del Vin, or near the *Erberia* (fruit-and-vegetable market) and the *Pescaria* (fish market), where the walkways border the water. Most of the other banks of the Grand Canal are inaccessible.**

Fondaco dei Turchi

The first building of note on the right bank is the **Fondaco dei Turchi**. Built in 1227 (though brutally restored in the 19th century), it is one of the grand canal's oldest survivors, once used as a trading base and living quarters for Turkish merchants. Nowadays it is home to the **Museo di Storia Naturale** (Natural History Museum, currently being restored, Sat–Sun 10am–4pm; tel, 041-275 0206), which is a rather old-fashioned collection but still a popular choice with children. Among the more terrifying exhibits are a monster crab with legs 2m (6½ft) long and a scorpion over 30cm (1ft) long. The most impressive exhibits, however, are in the dinosaur room, notably the bones of possibly the largest extinct crocodilian creatures ever found (measuring 11m/37ft in length) and the complete skeleton of a massive biped reptile known as an *ouranosaurus* (standing almost 3.5m/12ft high and some 7m/23ft long).

Just beyond the San Marcuola landing stage on the left bank is the **Palazzo Vendramin-Calergi**, designed by Mauro Coducci (1440–1504). It was here that the German composer Richard Wagner died in 1883; the building now provides an opulent setting for Venice's Casino *(see page 90)*.

Ca' Pesaro

Beyond the San Stae stop on the right bank is the vast baroque **Ca' Pesaro**, designed by Baldassare Longhena (the architect of the Salute). Decorated with grotesque masks, the Ca' (short for 'Casa', or house) was completed in 1682. Nowadays it houses the **Galleria Internazionale d'Arte Moderna** (open Tues–Sun 10am–6pm, until 5pm in winter; admission fee), which was founded with the best of the Biennale exhibition pieces and features mainly Italian artists, with a few important international contemporary works. Upstairs is the **Museo d'Arte Orientale** (same opening times as above), a rather confusing jumble of lacquered pieces, Samurai arms and armour and other artefacts given to Venice by Austria after World War I in preparation for bombing attacks on the city.

Ca' d'Oro

By the next landing stage is the **Ca' d'Oro** (open Mon 8.15am–2pm, Tues–Sun 8.15am–7.15pm; admission fee), built in the first quarter of the 15th century for the wealthy patrician Marino Contarini. The Ca' was originally covered in gold leaf, hence its name, which means 'House of Gold'. It is one of the most famous frontages on the Grand Canal, renowned for its elaborate Gothic façade decorated with magnificent tracery. Inside is the **Franchetti Gallery**, home to Mantegna's gruesome *St Sebastian*, depicting the saint riddled with arrows, some notable Renaissance sculpture, minor paintings by Tintoretto and Titian, and remnants of frescos recovered from other buildings, including some by Giorgione.

> 'A man's life often resembles these palaces on the Grand Canal, which begin at the base with an array of stones proudly sculpted in diamond points, and end with the upper floors hastily cobbled together from dry mud.'
> Paul Morand

Water markers, a frequent sight on the Venetian canals

Around the Rialto

Just north of the Rialto, on the left bank, stands the 13th-century Venetian-Byzantine-style **Ca' da Mosto**, one of the oldest houses on the canal. Nearby is the landmark **Ponte di Rialto** (Rialto Bridge, *see page 58*). Also on the left bank, to the south, are the handsome twin 13th-century *palazzi* **Loredan** and **Farsetti**, which now function as the town hall. Still on the left bank is the **Palazzo Mocenigo** complex, marked by blue-and-white mooring posts *(pali)*. The poet Lord Byron lived here from 1819 to 1824, while balancing the needs of a number of fiery local mistresses and working on his mock-heroic narrative poem *Don Juan*. Byron's most daring Venetian venture was to swim in a race against two other men from the Lido *(see page 84)* all the way to the Rialto – an excellent swimmer, the poet was the only one to finish. Today, the Grand Canal is no longer clean enough for such aquatic feats. .

The next building on the right bank is the splendid mid-13th-century **Palazzo Bernardo**, which may look familiar, since its tracery mirrors that of the Palazzo Ducale. On the same side, on the bend of the canal, look out for three attractive palaces: the **Balbi** (1590), then the **Ca' Foscari** (1437), currently home to the university, and finally the **Giustinian** (*c.*1452), where Wagner composed part of his opera *Tristan and Isolde*.

Ca' Rezzonico

Located a few blocks on is the glorious 17th-century **Ca' Rezzonico** (open Wed–Mon 10am–6pm; admission fee), home to the Museo del Settecento Veneziano (Museum of 18th-Century Venice), the third of Dorsoduro's major art collections. Here, however, the 17th-century palatial setting is just as important as the 18th-century exhibits it houses.

Ca' Rezzonico

Stepping into the Ca' Rezzonico is a feast for the eyes. At the top of the vast entrance staircase is a stunning ballroom, featuring two immense Murano-glass chandeliers as well as vibrantly decorated ceilings and walls. In the adjacent room are intricately carved figures of chained slaves.

Ceilings by Tiepolo (father and son) are the main

artistic interest until you reach the gallery on the second floor. Most visitors are immediately drawn to the two **Canaletto paintings** of the Grand Canal – note that there are only three paintings by him in Venice altogether. You'll also find works by **Pietro Longhi**, who recorded the final, decadent century of the Venetian Republic. On the third and fourth floors of the museum, the Gallery Egidio Martini showcases an impressive collection of around 300 works, mainly by Venetian painters.

The views from the windows overlooking the Grand Canal are also to be savoured. Pen Browning, the son of poet Robert Browning owned this palace in the late 19th century, and his father died in an apartment of the palace in 1889. The American-born artist James Whistler also lived here, from 1879 to 1880.

Towards the Ponte dell'Accademia

Opposite the Ca' Rezzonico is the 18th-century **Palazzo Grassi**, which until recently was owned by Fiat and used as a major art exhibition centre. It was bought by the French magnate, François Pinault, in 2005 to house his magnificent collection of modern art. (The palace is due to reopen in 2006.)

A little further on, the **Ponte dell'Accademia** (Accademia Bridge) was built as a temporary wooden arch in 1932, replacing an iron structure erected by the Austrians that had become an obstruction to larger *vaporetti*. The bridge is a favourite look-out point and has fine views over the Salute church.

The splendid building to the left, with the classic red-and-white *pali*, is the 15th-century **Palazzo Cavalli Franchetti**, while the neighbouring **Palazzi Barbaro**, built from the 15th to the 17th centuries, was much favoured by the artistic and literary set – writers Robert Browning and Henry James, and artists John Singer Sargent, Claude Monet and James Whistler all spent time here.

Towards Ca' Dario

Next en route is the right bank's **Palazzo Barbarigo,** decorated with strikingly gaudy, late-19th-century mosaics. Close by, the one-storey **Palazzo Venier dei Leoni** is home to the Collezione Peggy Guggenheim *(see page 51)*. The final building to note as you head along the canal is the gently listing 15th-century **Ca' Dario** (or Palazzo Dario), the former home of the Venetian chancery secretary, Giovanni Dario. Five centuries of scandal, from suicides to bankruptcy to suspicious deaths, have plagued the house. Note its funnel-shaped chimney pots, designed to reduce the risk of fire.

CANNAREGIO

This district, close to the railway station, is the most northerly one in Venice. Its name comes from *canne,* meaning reeds, indicating its marshy origins. This is an ancient quarter, often scorned by the snobbish in favour of the more stylish Dorsoduro *(see page 48)* – ironically, this was once one of the city's most fashionable spots, dotted with foreign embassies and palatial gardens. The palaces may be faded, but Cannaregio remains both a retreat for cognoscenti and the last bastion for working-class Venetians who have not moved to the Mestre mainland. It is also the site of the world's first Jewish ghetto.

Star of David from the Ghetto

The Ghetto

For almost 300 years, until Napoleon ended the practice in 1797, the Jews of Venice were permitted to live only in this tiny section of Cannaregio, surrounded on all sides

Mural in the Ghetto

by canals. The area had previously been a foundry or *ghetto* in Venetian; the word 'ghetto' subsequently came to denote Jewish and other segregated quarters all over the world.

Jewish refugees fleeing the War of Cambrai in 1508 came in their thousands to settle here. At the Ghetto's peak in the 17th century, its inhabitants numbered some 5,000, and the limited space led to the building of tenements six storeys high (still tall for Venice). Venetian Jews were severely taxed, forced to wear distinctive clothing, barred from many professions and made to observe a curfew, which was strictly enforced by gates and watchmen.

However, by the 16th century, the Ghetto was flourishing, with choirs, theatrical groups and literary salons that were visited by non-Jewish Venetians. The market at the Campo del Ghetto was the lively 'pawnshop of Venice' – an international attraction where treasures from the great houses of Venice's recently bankrupt or dead were bought and sold.

Today, the Ghetto is a quiet residential corner of Venice, with only a small Jewish population. The **Museo Ebraico** (Jewish Museum; open June–Sept Sun–Fri 10am–7pm; Oct–May Sun–Fri 10am–5.30pm; admission fee) contains a remarkable collection of Italian Judaica and runs tours of synagogues in the area every hour. On the opposite side of the square from the museum, a series of reliefs commemorates the 202 Venetian Jews who died during World War II.

VENETIAN CHURCHES

Venice's churches are full of treasures, so if you have more than a few days to spend, seek out some of the following.

Santi Giovanni e Paolo (San Zanipolo)

Commonly known as **San Zanipolo** (names are often slurred together in the Venetian dialect), this church (open Mon–Sat

St Dominic ceiling, San Zanipolo

7.30am–12.30pm and 3.30–7.30pm, Sun 3.30–7pm) is one of the largest in Venice after San Marco, disputing second place with its great Gothic sister, the Frari *(see page 61)*. Located on Campo Santi Giovanni e Paolo, in the Castello district, it was completed in 1430 for the Dominican Order and is known nowadays as Venice's Pantheon, as such a large number of doges (25 in all) and dignitaries of the Republic lie within. Like the

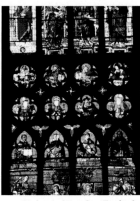

Stained glass, San Zanipolo

Frari, the church is cavernous, with graphic sculptures adorning its tombs. The church's treasures include an early polyptych by Giovanni Bellini in the right-hand nave.

San Zanipolo shares the *campo* with the late 15th-century Scuola Grande di San Marco (now a civic hospital) and a magnificent 15th-century equestrian statue of Bartolomeo Colleoni by Andrea Verrochio and Alessandro Leopardi. The subject is the mercenary military leader who worked in the service of Venice for many years and left a large legacy to the city on condition that his statue would be raised 'at the Square of San Marco'. The leaders of the Republic, who had never erected statues to any of their leaders or permitted cults of personality, wanted the legacy, but could not conceive of erecting a statue to a mercenary soldier – certainly not in Piazza San Marco. As a compromise, Colleoni's statue was placed in the square of the Scuola Grande di San Marco; the rather tenuous San Marco association presumably saved the municipal conscience.

Santa Maria dei Miracoli

Close to San Zanipolo, hidden amid a warren of canals and houses in the north of the Castello district, is the pretty little church of **Santa Maria dei Miracoli** – a popular choice for Venetian weddings. Built by the Lombardos, a family of inventive stonemasons (they created the *trompe-l'oeil* façade of the Scuola Grande di San Marco, *see previous page*), from 1481 to 1489, the church is notable for the exquisite marble veneers on its inner and outer walls and its arched ceiling, decorated with 50 portraits of prophets and saints.

Madonna dell'Orto

The 15th-century **Madonna dell'Orto** (Our Lady of the Garden; open 9.30am–noon and 3.30–5.30pm) occupies a quiet spot in Cannaregio, in the north of the city. The church, which has a delicate Gothic façade and lovely cloister, was built to house a miraculous statue of the Virgin and Child, found in a nearby garden *(orto)*. However, it is best known nowadays for its connections with the Renaissance painter Tintoretto – this was his parish church, and he is buried with his family to the right of the choir, near the high altar. The church is filled with Tintoretto's paintings, including his *Last Judgment*, *The Worship of the Golden Calf* and the *Presentation of the Virgin* (over the sacristy door), which demonstrates the artist's typical theatricality and grandiosity. Also of interest is Cima da Conegliano's remarkable painting of *St John the Baptist*, to the right of the entrance.

> Tintoretto (1518–94), who spent his whole life in Venice, was nicknamed after his father's trade as a dyer.

San Nicolò dei Mendicoli

Set behind the docks, in a quiet area of Dorsoduro, this humble parish church (open daily 10am–noon and

Taking a break from sightseeing

4–6pm) is often overlooked, but its relatively modest exterior belies its lavishly decorated interior. The church was founded in the 7th century, making it one of the oldest in the city, and remodelled between the 12th and 14th centuries; it was sensitively restored in 1977 by the Venice in Peril Fund *(see page 11)*. The church's single nave is graced by Romanesque columns, Gothic capitals and beamed ceilings, while decoration includes Renaissance panelling, gilded statues and paintings from the School of Veronese.

San Sebastiano

Also near the docks in Dorsoduro, the splendid 16th-century church of **San Sebastiano** (open Mon–Sat 10am–5pm, Sun 1–5pm; admission fee) is a glittering tribute to Veronese, who painted most of the opulent works decorating the walls, altar and ceiling from 1555 to 1565. The artist is also buried here; at present the church is undergoing continuing renovation.

San Giorgio Maggiore

THE ISLANDS

A highlight of any visit to Venice is a *vaporetto* trip through the inviting lagoon. Although many of its small islands are uninhabited wildernesses, inaccessible by public transport, there is a range of others to visit, from glass-making Murano to colourful Burano and serene Torcello. Here are some suggestions for leisurely half-day or one-day island excursions.

San Giorgio Maggiore

San Giorgio Maggiore is the closest island to the city, located almost within swimming distance of the Palazzo Ducale. The only major island of the lagoon that is untouched by commerce, it is home to a magnificent Palladian church/monastery and celebrated for the glorious views it affords back over the lagoon towards Venice. To reach the island, take the No 82 *vaporetto*; the journey lasts little more than 5 minutes.

Palladio's church (open daily 9.30am–12.30pm, 2.30–6.30pm; until 4.30pm in winter) was completed in 1610, and the result is a masterpiece of proportion and harmonious space. Tintoretto's *Last Supper* and *The Gathering of Manna* (both 1592–4) grace either side of the chancel. The high altar is dominated by a large bronze group by Girolamo Campagna and represents the evangelists sustaining the world. Behind are the church's splendidly carved 16th-century choir stalls.

For most visitors, however, the church takes second place to the view from its 200-year-old campanile (admission fee). Take the lift to the top for one of the great panoramas of Venice, then look down into the cloister of the **monastery** below to see a rare grassy space. The Fondazione Cini occupies much of the monastic complex. Guided tours are available at weekends, covering the library, refectory, cloisters and Teatro Verde, the open-air theatre (for bookings tel: 041-524 0119).

San Michele

The island of **San Michele** is the site of the city's cemetery, hence its sombre nickname, the 'island of the dead'. It lies 400 metres (440 yards) from Fondamente Nuove and is

Rest in Peace?

Nowhere is Venice's chronic lack of available land brought home so vividly as on the cemetery island of San Michele. In the early 1800s Napoleon decreed that burials should no longer take place in the city, and on San Michele they are not so much welcomed as tolerated. Burial lasts for ten years only, however, and unless the deceased has made provision for an extension on his or her lease – something that few Venetians can afford – then at the end of that time the remains are exhumed and sent to an ossuary to make way for the next occupant.

accessed by *vaporetti* Nos 41 and 42, which stop right outside **San Michele in Isola**, an elegant Renaissance church clad in glistening white Istrian stone.

Go through the cloister to reach the cemetery (open Apr–Sept daily 7.30am–6pm; Oct–Mar daily 7.30am–4pm). Among the cypress trees, you can visit the graves of American poet Ezra Pound (1885–1972), in section XV, and composer Igor Stravinsky (1882–1971) and impresario Serge Diaghilev (1872–1929), in section XIV.

Murano

After San Michele, the *vaporetto* stop at **Murano**, an island long famed for its glass-blowing tradition. Free water-taxi excursions are offered by glass factories or hotels, but if you want to avoid high-pressure sales tactics once you're on the island, take the *vaporetto* and make your own way around the factories instead. Orientation in Murano is a simple matter. From the main quay, where you disembark at the Colonna *vaporetto* stop, stroll along the picturesque Fondamenta dei Vetrai, which leads to Murano's very own Grand Canal.

Although glass was manufactured in Venice as far back as the 10th century, the open furnaces presented such a fire hazard that *c*.1292 the Republic ordered the factories to be transferred to Murano. Grouped here, the glass blowers kept the secrets of their trade for centuries; the manufacture of mirrors, for instance, was for a long time exclusive to Venice.

> It is thought that the Muranesi were the first to invent spectacles, in the early 14th century. By that time they were widely renowned for their window panes, which were the largest and clearest in Europe.

The island prospered, and by the early 16th century its population reached some 30,000. Glass artisans were considered honoured citi-

Contemporary Murano glass

zens. Murano's crystalware decorated royal palaces abroad, and its sumptuous villas housed the leading nobles and diplomats of the city. In time, as other countries learned and applied the secrets of Murano's glass-making, the island's importance declined, and by the 19th century most of its grand summer residences were no more. However, the glass industry was revived later that century and continues today, though not always up to the old standards and often at over-inflated prices. However, a number of contemporary glass workshops still create outstanding designs.

For an interesting review of the history of Venetian glass, visit the **Museo del Vetro** (Glass Museum; open Thurs–Tues, Apr–Oct 10am–5pm, Nov–Mar 10am–4pm; admission fee), housed in a 17th-century bishop's palace on Fondamente Giustinian.

Nearby, on Campo San Donato, is the church of **Santi Maria e Donato** (open daily 8.30am–noon, 3.30–6pm), which is possibly the oldest church in Venice – its 7th-century foundations may predate the Basilica di San Marco. The church is splendidly atmospheric, and both the brightly coloured 12th-century mosaic floor and a golden mosaic of the Madonna over the high altar have been restored with great care and sympathy. While you're in the church, note the giant bones behind the altar; these are said to be those of a dragon slain by St Donato. Unlike St George, Donato eschewed the conventional lance and sword, slewing the beast simply by spitting at it.

Burano

The LN (Laguna Nord) ferry service to **Burano** leaves roughly every half hour from Venice's Fondamente Nuove; those visiting from Murano can pick the ferry up at the Faro (lighthouse) stop. The journey to Burano and the neighbouring island of Torcello takes around 45 minutes.

Burano is a friendly, colourful island which feels like an authentic old fishing village. Its buildings are painted in a rainbow of blue, red, peppermint, russet and yellow, and these colours all reflect in the waters of the canals. You won't need a map here – it's such a small place that you're unlikely to get lost if you use the campanile of San Martino *(see opposite)* as your reference point.

The island once produced the world's finest lace, and its exquisitely light *punto in aria* pattern was the most sought after in Europe. Nowadays, the lace you see in local shops is largely imported from Asia, and real Burano lace is created by only a handful of women trained at the island's special **Scuola del Merletto** (School of Lacemaking; open Wed–Mon 10am–5pm, until 4pm in winter; admission fee), on Piazza Galuppi. The school was opened in 1872 to re-train the island's women at a time when the numbers of skilled lacemakers had dwindled to just one.

Before leaving the square, visit the 16th-century church of **San Martino** (open daily 8am–noon and 3–6pm), famous for its 18th-century leaning campanile. San Martino is also home to the island's only major art treasure: Tiepolo's *Crucifixion*.

San Francesco del Deserto

From Burano, the peaceful island of **San Francesco del Deserto** makes a lovely detour. The trip takes about 20 minutes and can normally be arranged with a boatman on Burano's main square. St Francis is said to have landed on the island in 1220, on his return from the Holy Land, and Franciscan friars have been here almost ever since. A handful of the brethren choose to make this a permanent home, while young novices spend a year here as part of their training. The monastery (open Tues–Sat 9–11am and 3–5pm, Sun 3–5pm) has a beautiful 14th-century cloister and gardens.

Burano waterfront

Torcello

The long boat trip to **Torcello** helps the visitor to appreciate the remoteness of this evocative island. Amazing as it seems now, in early medieval times this overgrown, almost deserted island was the lagoon's principal city, with an estimated population of 20,000. However, with the silting up of its canals into marshes, a consequent outbreak of malaria and then the ascendancy of Venice, there was a mass exodus from the island. Today, there are only about 50 inhabitants on Torcello.

As you walk from the *vaporetto* stage to the cathedral, the canal is the only familiarly Venetian feature. On Torcello, buildings have given way to trees, fields and thick undergrowth. The novelist George Sand captured the pastoral mood of her visit in the 1830s, 'Torcello is a reclaimed wilderness. Through copses of water willow and hibiscus bushes run saltwater streams where petrel and teal delight to stalk.'

The solitary path leads past the ancient **Ponte del Diavolo** to a small square where Torcello's cathedral, the adjacent church of Santa Fosca and the Museo di Torcello (Torcello Museum) all stand. The Italian-Byzantine cathedral **Santa Maria dell'Assunta** (open daily 10.30am–6pm, 5pm in winter; admission fee, collective ticket available) was founded in AD639, but dates mostly from 1008, and is therefore the oldest monument in the lagoon. Among the cathedral's treasures is its original 7th-century altar and a Roman sarcophagus containing the relics of St Heliodorus, first Bishop of Altinum (where the island's first settlers were originally from).

Symbolic statuary

Mosaic, Santa Maria Assunta

Also among the cathedral's highlights are its rich **mosaics**, judged by many to be the finest in Italy outside those at Ravenna. A masterpiece of Byzantine design adorns the central apse: a slender, mysterious *Madonna*, bathed in a cloth of gold. At the opposite end of the building, an entire wall is covered by a complex, heavily restored *Last Judgement*, probably begun early in the 12th century. The steep climb up the campanile will reward you with a panoramic view of the lagoon.

Santa Fosca (open daily 10am–12.30pm and 2–5pm), built in the 11th and 12th centuries and harmoniously combining Romanesque and Byzantine elements, has a bare simplicity rarely found in Venetian churches, while the **Museo dell'Estuario** (same hours as cathedral, *see page 82*) houses a collection of architectural details from long-disappeared local churches and other buildings. Outside the museum, note the primitive stone chair, known as 'Attila's Throne'; it is possibly an early judge's seat.

Thomas Mann

The Lido

The long strip of land, sand-wiched between the city of Venice and the waters of the Adriatic, belongs neither to Venice nor the mainland. This reflects the Lido's prime function: to protect Venice from the engulfing tides. In spirit, it is a place apart, not quite a traditional summer resort nor a residential sub-

Death in Venice

Death and Venice go together, with the lagoon a familiar backdrop to modern murder mysteries. The city's taste for the macabre is partly a romanticised notion fed by visions of sinister alleys, the inkiness of a lagoon night or a *cortège* of mourning gondolas gliding across the water. However, Venetian history does provide tales of murdered Doges and deadly plots nipped in the bud by the secret police.

And the most celebrated work of literature set in Venice, Thomas Mann's novella *Death in Venice*, does little to dispel the myth. The book follows the decline of the writer Gustav von Aschenbach – a man who believes that art is produced only in 'defiant despite' of corrupting passions and physical weakness. On a reluctant break from work, Aschenbach finds himself in Venice, which Mann depicts as a place of decadence and spiritual dislocation. Aschenbach's obsession with a beautiful Polish boy staying at his hotel (the Lido's Hotel des Bains) has dire consequences, as he becomes a slave to his passions, ignoring a cholera epidemic that the corrupt Venetian authorities try to conceal.

urb. After the time warp of historic Venice, the sight of cars, large villas and department stores can be disconcerting. Yet there is a touch of unreality about the Lido, as there is about Venice itself, hence its frequent role as a film set. In this faded fantasy, neo-Gothic piles vie with Art Nouveau villas and a mock-Moorish castle.

The Lido's Hotel des Bains

Since the Lido cannot compete with the historical riches of the rest of Venice, it generally remains the preserve of residents and visitors staying on the island. Although most day-trippers stray no further than the smart hotels and the beaches where the poets Byron and Shelley once raced on horseback, the Lido offers subtle pleasures for those willing to look, from belle époque architecture to a delightful cycle ride along the sea walls to Malamocco.

The ferries from San Marco deposit visitors among the traffic at the edge of the shopping district. Close to the jetties stands the 16th-century church of **Santa Maria Elisabetta**; behind is the main street, Gran Viale Santa Maria Elisabetta, which cuts across the island from the lagoon shore to the Adriatic. At the far end of the Viale lies the Lungomare, the seafront promenade and the focus of the summer evening *passeggiata* (promenade). Beyond are the best Adriatic beaches, private pockets of sand bedecked with colourful cabins.

The Lido is home to several of the city's most elegant hotels, including the palatial Hotel des Bains, which helped to inspire Thomas Mann's *Death in Venice (see box opposite)*.

WHAT TO DO

ENTERTAINMENT

For visitors in search of cultural entertainment Venice can't be faulted, with year-round classical concerts, opera, theatre, art exhibitions and festivals to suit all tastes. Nightlife of the clubbing, pubbing kind rates less well, due to a large degree to the fact that the average age in Venice is 45. What late-night entertainment there is tends to be low key, focused on piano bars, the historic cafés around San Marco and chic hotel bars. Recently, however, the nightlife scene has been livened up with a number of hip late-night lounge bars. For that authentic Venetian experience, traditional bars known as *bacari (see page 100)* are certainly worth a visit.

The Performance Arts

The most popular venues for **classical-music concerts**, from organ recitals to choral works, are Venice's many churches, especially San Bartolomeo, Santo Stefano, the Frari, San Vidal and the Salute; the Scuole (charitable confraternities) are also important venues for music of this kind. To the chagrin of the locals, there tends to be a preponderance of groups specialising in Venice's very own Antonio Vivaldi, although most give highly accomplished performances. The chamber group Interpreti Veneziani (<www.interpretiveneziani.com>) is a good name to look for. A number of ensembles, including I Musici Veneziani and Orchestra di Venezia, a Baroque chamber orchestra, perform in costume. For details of what's on when, check Venice's comprehensive listings magazine, *Un Ospite di Venezia*, available at many hotels. The website <www.meeting venice.it> also has information on performances and events.

Opera in Venice has a rather tragic history – the city's main opera house, **La Fenice** (The Phoenix), on Campo San

Fantin, once dubbed 'the prettiest theatre in Europe', was badly damaged by fire in 1996 – its third fire since its construction in 1774. It finally reopened in 2004 with a triumphant performance of Verdi's *La Traviata* (tel: 041-786511; <www.teatrolafenice.it>). The opera season runs from November until May.

Another attractive venue for opera is the Teatro Malibran (Cannaregio 5873, tel: 041-786 764), a tiny jewel of a theatre that reopened in 2001 after 10 years of restoration. Dating from 1678, when it was known as Il Teatro di San Giovanni Grisostomo, the building was renamed in the 19th century when it was dedicated to a celebrated diva, Maria Malibran. Opera fans may also be interested in the summer programme at the nearby Arena di Verona.

For drama, try the **Teatro Goldoni** (San Marco 4650), which offers a year-round programme of plays performed by Italian and international companies, some with translations.

Carnevale

The black cloak, tricorn hat, white mask and other rather sinister garb identified with Venice's Carnevale date back the 18th century when the *commedia dell'arte* was in vogue. In the final century of the decadent, drifting Republic, Carnevale was extended to six months, and Venetians wore these costumes from December to June. Under this guise of anonymity, commoner and aristocrat were interchangeable, husbands and wives could pursue amours unchallenged, and all sorts of misdemeanors could be committed. Things got so out of hand that Carnevale was eventually banned. Today's Carnevale, revived only in 1979 and held in February/March, is more restrained. Nonetheless, this is one time of year that the city really comes to life, with street parties, masked balls, pageants, special events and visitors from all over Europe. Contact the tourist office *(see page 125–6)* for details.

La Biennale

Venice's Biennale is one of
the oldest, most important
exhibitions of contemporary
art in the world. Established
in 1895 to celebrate a royal
silver wedding anniversary,
it has been held regularly
ever since. Nowadays it
takes place in odd years,
(the architectural Biennale
is held on even years) between June and November,

Culture fatigue

in the 40 pavilions of the Gardini Pubblici, and the restored
Corderie (rope factory) and other warehouses of the Arsenale. Each pavilion is sponsored by a different country, offering a chance for avant-garde art, often with wry political
comment, to be displayed.

Clubs and Bars

With Venice's elderly resident population and large number
of day-trippers, nightlife of this kind is somewhat restrained. However, if you're prepared to venture away from
Piazza San Marco, you'll be rewarded with a scattering of
late-night bars, mostly frequented by students and young
Venetians; there are details of these in *Un Ospite di Venezia*, *Venezia News* and the booklet produced by Rolling
Venice *(see pages 118 and 126)*. Dorsoduro, with its student district, is home to the best night spots, including **Pic-
colo Mondo** (1056a Dorsoduro), an off-beat place with a
mixed clientele, and the lively late-night bars and cafés in
Campo Santa Margherita. **Margaret DuChamp** is a fashionable bar on the square, and **Orange** is a contemporary
lounge bar with an in-house DJ. **Bistrot de Venise** (Calle

dei Fabbri 4685, San Marco) is a rare eatery that stays open very late and organises concerts and poetry recitals on certain nights. Close to Piazza San Marco, **Bacaro Lounge** in Salizzada San Moisè is a hip cocktail bar with jazz music and a restaurant.

The Casino

Venice's municipal **Casinò** (tel: 041-529 7111) is held in the Palazzo Vendramin-Calergi on the Grand Canal. Games, including roulette, chemin de fer, baccarat and blackjack, are played until the early hours. A passport is essential for admittance to the gambling rooms, as are jackets and ties for men.

Film

Most foreign films shown in Italy are dubbed into Italian. *Versione originale* (original version) or *VO* indicates that films are presented in their own language.

Although generally seen as less prestigious than the Cannes Festival International du Film, the Venice Film Festival (Mostra Internazionale d'Arte Cinematografica) is still a major event on the international cinema circuit, lasting for 2 weeks in late August/early September. At this balmy time of the year, the city welcomes the stars, who can be seen parading along the seafront or sipping Bellinis on the grand terrace of the Excelsior Hotel, where the first film festival (reputedly also the world's first, predating Cannes by 14 years) opened in 1932. Founded as a showcase for Fascist Italy, the festival's success belies its unpromising origins.

The stress is now on arthouse, rather than blockbuster, films – a policy that the Venetians hope will boost the ailing Italian film industry. It's usually difficult for visitors outside the film and press industries to attend the festival, but for

The Grand Canal at night

information, check <www.labiennale.org>. If you want to chance your luck, the action is centred around the Lido by day and San Marco by night.

SHOPPING

One of the most satisfying aspects of shopping in Venice is separating the treasure-house from the tourist trap. As a general rule, the luxury-end shops (jewellery, glassware, leather, etc) are located around Piazza San Marco. However, this area is also home to a proliferation of tacky tourist shops, offering overpriced souvenirs.

For less tourist-orientated purchases, head for the Strada Nuova, which leads behind the Ca' d'Oro towards the railway station. The odd bargain can be found in artisans' workshops on the Giudecca and in the Dorsoduro behind the Zattere, while a cross-section of Venetian craftsmanship can be had for more affordable prices at the artisans' shops on the Frezzeria.

For fashion, the shopping street of Mercerie (described in 1645 by John Evelyn as 'the most delicious streete in the world') has quality boutiques, which become increasingly affordable the further away from Piazza San Marco you head.

Glassware

Contemporary Venetian glassware poses a problem of quality and price, so hunt carefully. The factories on Murano rarely offer better prices than shops in mainland Venice, but they will give free demonstrations and transport to the island. When choosing gifts to be shipped, bypass the extremely fragile items and always ask for handling and insurance rates before you buy, as they may double the price. For more information, visit <www.muranoglass.com>.

Lace

The small museum on Burano is the best place to see intricate laceware being made in the traditional manner. The real thing is exquisite but exorbitantly priced, with many lesser-quality, machine-made pieces from the Far East being passed off as locally hand-made. If you don't have time to visit Burano, you can buy modern reproductions and interpretations of traditional patterns around San Marco.

Murano glass

Marbled Paper

Venice is also famed for its marbled paper, made by a process known as *legatoria* or 'book-binding'. A special mixture is spread on the paper, then wavy patterns, like peacock's feathers, are created by teasing a comb through the mixture. Paper of this kind used to be popular for binding books and pamphlets and as a background for documents, thus providing protection against forgery. Today, it is used mainly to make photograph albums, writing cases, greeting cards and notebooks.

Luxury leather

Tax

IVA (value-added tax) is added into prices on a sliding scale, reaching 19 percent. Non-EU citizens are entitled to a refund of this tax on purchases of €180 or more, if made in one place; ask for an invoice from the seller. Save receipts until you leave your last EU destination. Look out for shops offering tax-free shopping for tourists; they usually deduct this tax on the spot.

SPORTS

Venice itself offers few leisure facilities for the sporty visitor, except for two **public pools**: one by the Sacca Fissola *vaporetto* stop on the Giudecca, the other by the stop at Sant'Alvise. At the end of each October, the city hosts a world-class **marathon** that attracts more than 6,000 runners from across the world. If you want to participate, contact your local running club for details or visit <www.venicemarathon.it>.

   A more relaxed option for holidaying sports lovers is a trip to the Lido, where, from June to September, most of the private beaches of the large hotels offer a variety of water sports, including **windsurfing**, **water-skiing**, **canoeing** and dinghy and catamaran **sailing**. However, swimming is not always permitted on the Lido's beaches due to pollution problems. Dry-land

Sunbathing on the Lido

sporting opportunities on the Lido include 18-hole golf at Alberoni-Lido (course open all year round, with clubs for hire) and, in summer, tennis clubs open to the public.

Knowledge of the lagoon's channels is necessary for safe boating, so motorboats are not rented out to tourists. However, if you belong to a rowing club at home and can produce proof of membership, one of the local rowing clubs may let you join their ranks. Contact the Società Cannottieri Bucintoro, Zattere, 15, Dorsoduro (tel: 041-520 5630, <www.bucintoro.org>).

VENICE FOR CHILDREN

The waterways of Venice never fail to impress the young at heart, making a gondola ride *(see page 55)* a good choice for parents in search of family entertainment. However, if the inflated cost of a gondola brings tears to your eyes, simply take the kids on a *vaporetto* – Venice's waterbuses offer the distinct advantage that children under 4 years of age travel free, and there are reduced fares for families. Excursions to the Lido, where there are beaches and 'water banana' rides and pedalos, are always popular with children in summer.

Cultural options include: excursions to Murano to watch glass-blowers at their craft *(see page 78)*; a visit to the Museo Storico Navale *(see page 47)*, home to a fascinating array of ship models and life-size ships; and a trip up the Campanile di San Marco *(see page 25)*, for enticing views across the city. Finally, consider planning your trip to coincide with July's Festa del Redentore with its fabulous fireworks *(see opposite)*.

Festivals and Events

1 January *Capodanno* (New Year's Day). Public holiday. Beach celebrations.

February/March *Carnevale* (Carnival). Ten-day, pre-Lenten extravaganza with masked balls, processions, pantomime and music.

Easter Monday *Lunedi di Pasqua*. Public holiday. Date varies.

25 April *Anniversario della Liberazione* (Liberation Day). Public holiday.

25 April *Festa di San Marco* (St Mark's Day). Ceremonial Mass in the Basilica, when rosebuds *(bocolo)* are given as love tokens. A gondola race is also held between Sant'Elena and the Punta della Dogana, followed by a traditional meal of *risi e bisi* ('rice and peas'), actually a kind of soup.

Sunday after Ascension *La Sensa*, celebrating Venice's 'marriage with the sea'. Re-enacts trips made to the Lido by the doges, who cast rings into the water to symbolise the union of the Republic and its acquatic surroundings.

Two Sundays after Ascension *La Vogalonga* (literally: 'long row'). Hundreds of rowing boats follow a 32-km (20-mile) course from the Basino di San Marco to Burano and then San Francesco del Deserto.

June Odd years only (Jun–Sept). Biennale d'Arte. International art exhibition.

July, third Sunday *Festa del Redentore* (Festival of the Redeemer). Regatta with fireworks and festivities around the Lido.

August For two weeks, from late August until early September, Venice hosts its International Film Festival *(see page 90)* at the Lido.

15 August *Ferragosto* (Assumption). Public holiday. Concerts on Torcello.

September, first Sunday *La Regata Storica* (Historical Regatta) The finest regatta of the year, which begins with a procession up the Grand Canal led by costumed Venetians, followed by gondola races.

November Start of the opera season (runs until May).

1 November *Ognissanti* (All Saints' Day). Public holiday.

21 November *Festa della Salute*. Processions to the candlelit Santa Maria della Salute, commemorating the city's deliverance from the plague of 1630.

8 December *Festa della Madonna Immacolata* (Immaculate Conception). Public holiday.

25 December *Natale* (Christmas Day). Public holiday.

26 December *Santo Stefano* (Boxing Day). Public holiday.

EATING OUT

Most Venetians have traditional attitudes with regard to their food, and the city's restaurants reflect this, focussing on Venetian and other Italian dishes. There is little in the way of international cuisine, except for a handful of Italian-influenced Chinese restaurants and a few attempts at French cuisine in the more expensive hotels. Venetian food is heavily influenced by the bounty of the lagoon, with fresh fish, clams, shrimps, calamari, *seppie* (cuttlefish) and octopus all main features on the menu; duck and game birds, which inhabit the marshy islands, are also popular.

WHERE TO EAT

The San Marco area is awash with overpriced tourist-traps that no culinary-aware Venetian would consider frequenting. Most of the city's best restaurants are in the Dorsoduro, San Polo and Santa Croce neighbourhoods, just across the Grand Canal from San Marco. In theory, the word *ristorante* usually indicates a large, elaborate establishment, whereas a *trattoria* is a cosy, perhaps family-run, place and an *osteria* has a rustic atmostphere. Yet in Venice, as elsewhere in Italy, the distinction is often blurred beyond all recognition. Price should not be taken as an indication of quality – an expensive restaurant may offer a superb meal with service to match, but you will pay for the location. That said, there are still some fabulous top-notch restaurants here for those wishing to push the boat out.

Around San Marco, many restaurants offer a *menù turistico*, a fixed-price set menu. Although this may appear to be cheaper than eating *à la carte*, portions will invariably be smaller and the choice limited. If you are on a budget, you will get good value for money at a *pizzeria*, where pasta and traditional fish and meat dishes are often served as well as pizzas.

Italian restaurants have to display the menu with prices in the window or just inside the door, so you will have an idea of what's offered before you take the plunge. By law all restaurants (and bars) must issue a receipt from the cash register indicating that IVA (value-added tax) has been included. The bill usually includes service *(servizio)* of between 10 and 15 percent, but ask if you're not sure. It's normal to round the bill up slightly in addition to this. Meal times are from noon to 2.30 or 3pm, and from around 7.30 to 10pm.

VENETIAN CUISINE

Most Venetians start the day with *piccola colazione* – a coffee (a strong dark *espresso* or a foaming milky cappuccino) and a bread roll or croissant *(cornetto)*; the best place for this is a *caffè*. Remember that in a bar what you consume will cost twice as much if you eat it sitting at a table than standing at

Eating al fresco on Piazza San Marco

the bar. If you're breakfasting in a hotel, the larger chains usually serve an English- or American-style buffet.

For a quick snack at lunchtime, choose a *tavola calda*, a stand-up bar serving a variety of hot and cold dishes to take away or eat on the spot. For a larger meal, at both lunch *(pranzo)* and dinner *(cena)* there is generally a choice of four courses: *antipasti* (starters or appetisers); *primo piatto* (first course); *secondo piatto* (main course) with *contorni* (vegetable or salad accompaniments) and *dolce* (dessert). Don't worry if you're just looking for a light bite – you certainly won't be expected to order all four courses.

Appetizing salami

Appetisers

Any *trattoria* worth its olive oil will set out an artistic display of its *antipasti*, either vegetarian, fish-based or meaty, on a table near the entrance. A popular vegetarian choice is *carciofi* (artichokes), while those with fish include: *sarde in saor* (marinated sardines and onions, with pine kernels and raisins); *frutti di mare* (seafood), prawns, baby octopus, mussels and squid in a lemon dressing; and *vongole, caparozzoli* (both types of clam) or *cozze* (mussels), in a white-wine sauce. Meaty *antipasti* include *carpaccio*, thin slices of raw beef served with mayonnaise; *prosciutto crudo con melone* (ham with melon), sometimes offered with figs *(fichi)*; and *affettati* or spicy *salsicce* (charcuterie and salami-style sausage).

Colourful pasta varieties

First Course
The *primo piatto* is usually pasta, risotto or soup. This far north, pasta often takes second place to rice, and risotto is often recognised as *the* classic Venetian dish. Its constituents, apart from rice, are usually fresh vegetables or seafood. Venice's most famous pasta dish is *bigoli in salsa* (noodles in an anchovy sauce). *Zuppa di pesce* (a stew-like fish soup) is usually a good choice. *Pasta e fagioli* is a delicious thick, northern Italian pasta-and-white-bean soup.

Main Course
Seafood: Seafood dominates the *secondo piatto*, and *griglia-ta dell'Adriatico* or *frittura/fritto misto* (Adriatic grill or mixed fried fish) are two favourite Venetian dishes. Fish that feature heavily on menus here include *rombo* (turbot), *coda di rospo* (monkfish), *orata* (gilt-head bream), *branzino/spigo-la* (sea-bass), *San Pietro* (John Dory) and *sogliola* (sole). Local seafood favourites are *granceola* (spidercrab served in its own shell), *anguilla alla veneziana* (eel cooked in a sauce made with lemon, oil and tuna) and *seppie al nero* (cuttlefish in its own ink); this last is traditionally served with *polenta*, a firm, yellow cornmeal purée.
Meat: The city's most frequently cooked meat dish is *fegato alla veneziana* (calf's liver with onions), served with polenta.

Vitello tonnato (thin slices of cold veal fillet in tuna sauce) is also a good dish to try. The best restaurants pride themselves on their Aberdeen-Angus cuts, while Venice's *bistecca alla fiorentina* (Florentine T-bone steak) is, ironically, Italy's finest.

Vegetables/Salads: *Rucola* (rocket) and *radicchio* (a type of chicory from Treviso) are popular components of salads, while assorted grilled vegetables are common side dishes.

Desserts and Cheese

The dessert choice is often limited to around half a dozen items, including *gelato* (ice-cream) and *tiramisù* (literally 'pick me up'), a chilled coffee-flavoured, trifle-like confection. *Panna cotta* ('cooked cream') has a similar texture

---

Cichetti and Ombre

If you want to eat economically and try as many local delicacies as possible, look out for *bacari*, or tradional wine bars; these have counters of *cichetti* (plates of snacks, similar to *tapas*), from herbed shelled lobster claws drizzled with olive oil, to smoky grilled *calamari* and *pizzette* (tiny pizzas). At most bars, cafés, and *bacari*, there is no seating – everyone simply stands and nibbles the snacks with a glass of house wine in hand – even if there is seating, remember that food costs up to twice as much if you sit down, so most Venetians stand at the bar anyway.

Un ombrà (literally, 'shade') is the Venetian term for house wine, a phrase that comes from the fact that the locals 'step into the shade' when they break for a glass of wine. *Ombra di rosso* is the house red, *ombra di bianco* the house white.

Venice's most famous wine bar is Cantina do Mori on Calle do Mori near the Rialto Bridge. Founded in 1462, it's a dark place, crammed with brass pots. It serves fabulous *cichetti* and a variety of Veneto wines.

to crème caramel, but a
lighter taste. A typical
Venetian custom is to serve
vino dolce con biscotti, a
glass of dessert wine with
sweet biscuits.

Cheese: Strong *gorgonzola*
is popular, often served
with *parmigiano* or *grana*
(both parmesan). Among
the delicacies of the Veneto
province is a savoury,
tangy cow's milk cheese
named after the mountain
town of Asiago.

Italian staple

Snacks

The city's many bars and cafés offer stacks of assorted
tramezzini (white bread sandwiches, which are usually
heavy on the mayonnaise) and *panini* (filled rolls). For
tapas-style snacks, try *bacari (see box opposite)*.

DRINKS

Most restaurants offer the open wine of the house, red or
white, in $^1/_4$-litre, $^1/_2$-litre or 1-litre carafes, as well as a good
selection of bottled vintages. Many Veneto wines, including
Soave, *Valpolicella* and *Bardolino*, will probably be familiar,
thanks to their export success. Less well known is the local
wine region of Friuli, which supplies good *Pinot Grigio*, as
well as palatable house wines *(vini della casa)*. To widen
your knowledge of the local wines, look out for an *enoteca*, a
combination of bar and wine retailer.

Two sparkling drinks, consumed in cafés all over town,
are Prosecco, a great sparkling white wine, and *spritz*, a

combination of Campari, white wine and sparkling mineral water. Venice's other drink of note is the *Bellini*, an ambrosial concoction of Prosecco and fresh peach juice. It was invented by Signor Cipriani, the father of the current proprietor of Harry's Bar *(see page 139)*, the city's most famous (and most expensive) restaurant and night spot.

Bitters such as Campari and Punt e Mes are refreshing appetisers with soda and lemon. For after-dinner drinks, the options range from throat-warming *vecchia romagna* brandy, to sweet *strega*, almond-flavoured *amaretto*, aniseed-tasting *sambuca* and fiery *grappa* – there is no specifically Venetian *digestif.* For beer-drinkers, Nastro Azzuro is a national favourite; this brew, which is not as strong as most north European brands, is usually served refreshingly ice cold.

Non-alcoholic drinks range from wonderfully potent coffees and frothy hot chocolate to refreshing iced tea. Mineral water *(acqua minerale)* is a normal accompaniment to a meal – for sparkling, ask for *gasata*; still is *naturale.* Tap water in Venice is safe to drink unless marked *acqua non potabile.* The water from the many drinking fountains around the city is also perfectly safe.

Pizza

Pizza is in reality a much more elaborate affair than you may be used to – the classic 'Margherita', created in 1889 by a Neapolitan chef for Queen Margherita of Savoy, has tomato sauce and melted mozzarella. Toppings can include tomato, ham, anchovies, cheese, mushrooms, peppers, artichoke hearts, zucchini flowers, potatoes, egg, clams, tuna, garlic or any other ingredient that takes the cook's fancy. Note that in the summer *pizzerie* are not usually open for lunch – the high temperatures of their ovens and the midday heat would simply be overwhelming.

To Help You Order...

Waiters are called *cameriere* (men) or *cameriera* (women).
Do you have a set menu? **Avete un menù a prezzo fisso?**
I'd like a/an/some... **Vorrei...**

beer	**una birra**	pepper	**del pepe**
bread	**del pane**	potatoes	**delle patate**
butter	**del burro**	salad	**un'insalata**
coffee	**un caffè**	salt	**del sale**
cream	**della panna**	soup	**una minestra**
fish	**del pesce**	sugar	**dello zucchero**
fruit	**della frutta**	tea	**un tè**
ice-cream	**un gelato**	water	**dell'acqua**
meat	**della carne**	(mineral)	**(minerale)**
milk	**del latte**	wine	**del vino**

...and Read the Menu

aglio	garlic	**manzo**	beef
agnello	lamb	**mela**	apple
albicocche	apricots	**melanzane**	aubergine
aragosta	lobster	**merluzzo**	cod
arancia	orange	**ostriche**	oysters
bistecca	beefsteak	**pesca**	peach
braciola	chop	**piselli**	peas
calamari	squid	**pollo**	chicken
carciofi	artichokes	**pomodori**	tomatoes
cipolle	onions	**prosciutto**	ham
crostacei	shellfish	**rognoni**	kidneys
fegato	liver	**tacchino**	turkey
fichi	figs	**tonno**	tuna
formaggio	cheese	**uovo**	egg
frutti di mare	seafood	**uva**	grapes
funghi	mushrooms	**verdure**	vegetables
lamponi	raspberries	**vitello**	veal
maiale	pork	**vongole**	clams

HANDY TRAVEL TIPS

An A–Z Summary of Practical Information

A

ACCOMMODATION (For RECOMMENDED HOTELS, see page 128)

Venice is home to some of Europe's finest hotels as well as the more basic of dormitories. If there is one common factor it is that, like the city, most of the accommodation is old and characterful.

Hotels. Many of the city's hotels *(alberghi)* are housed within old palaces. When making reservations, ask for a room with a view, and, when checking in, ask to see a number of different rooms, as the quality can vary greatly within any one establishment. If your budget allows, plump for a room at attic level with a private roof deck – if your hotel has an elevator and air-conditioning attic rooms are easy to access, nice and cool and, basically, glorious. As a general rule, the nearer to Piazza San Marco a hotel is, the more expensive it will be. If you're looking for something slightly more economical, try across the Grand Canal in Dorsoduro or the less chic area of the Lista di Spagna near the railway station.

Hotels are graded from 5-star deluxe to 1-star; for a list of hotels with star ratings, visit the tourist office *(see pages 125–6)* or consult <www.turismovenezia.it>. You can book online through the Hoteliers' Association website, <www.veneziasi.it>. For a list of recommended hotels, *see page 128*. Hotel rates usually include continental breakfast, but most top-class and many moderate-range hotels serve more elaborate buffet breakfasts. In budget hotels, always check to see if there's air-conditioning, and, if there is, whether there is an extra charge for it.

Advance booking is essential during peak periods, from spring to autumn, around Christmas week and during Carnival; prices are at a premium at these times. However, in the chill of winter and sometimes during the sweltering mid-summer period (July and August), when the city's tourism is largely made up of day-trippers, it can be easier and more affordable to get a room. Prices can drop by as much as 50 percent in winter. Note that many Lido hotels are only open from April to October.

Budget accommodation. Below the 1-star category there are a few budget hostels *(ostelli)* and dormitory accommodation. The tourist office can supply a list of such places. The Instituto Canossiane (Fondamenta delle Romite, 30123 Dorsoduro, tel: 041-2409713) is an old convent with student accommodation.

Do you have any vacancies?	**Avete camere libere?**
I'd like a single/double room	**Vorrei una camera singola/ matrimoniale**
with (without) bath/shower	**con (senza) bagno/doccia**
What's the rate per night?	**Qual è il prezzo per una notte?**

AIRPORTS *(Aeroporti)*

Two airports serve Venice: Marco Polo and Treviso.

Venice Marco Polo is Venice's main airport, located 13 km (8 miles) north of the city. It has a new terminal and sports all the usual amenities expected of an international airport, including hotel and tourist-information booths, bank and currency-exchange offices *(cambio)*, restaurants, shops and internet access. Assistance for wheelchair travellers is available. For flight information, tel: 041-2609240 or visit <www.veniceairport.it>.

Public buses (ACTV) run from the airport to the terminus at Piazzale Roma every half-hour in summer and about once an hour in winter; **airport buses** (ATVO) have a similar timetable. Both are inexpensive (the ACTV service is the cheaper of the two, but very awkward if you have luggage) and take around 30 minutes to reach Piazzale Roma. Buy your tickets from ATVO office in the arrivals terminal. Once at Piazzale Roma (in Santa Croce, just across the Grand Canal from the train station), board the No. 1 *vaporetto* (waterbus) for an all-stages ride along the Grand Canal; take the No. 82 if you just want the quickest route to San Marco.

The Alilaguna water launches provide a year-round direct service between Marco Polo airport and central Venice. The Linea Rossa (Red Line) stops at Murano, Lido, Arsenale, San Marco and Zattere (Dorsoduro); the service runs roughly hourly from 6.15am until after midnight. The Linea Azzurra (Blue Line) stops at Murano, Fondamenta Nuove, Lido, Riva degli Schiavoni and San Marco; it runs hourly from 9.40am–10.40pm. The new Alilaguna Oro (Gold Line) Service goes direct to San Marco and takes one hour, saving about 15 minutes. This premium service costs €25 for a single journey compared to €10 on the Red or Blue lines. A free shuttle bus links the new airport terminal with the water launch pier.

Private **water taxis** *(taxi acquei)* are the fastest means to reach the centre (30 mins) but are very expensive, so be careful not to confuse them with the Alilaguna craft *(see above)*. However, they will take you right up to your hotel if it has a water entrance, or drop you off as close as possible.

Treviso is a small airport 30km (20 miles) north of Venice, used mainly by charter companies and low-cost airlines, who often, confusingly, call it 'Venice airport'. ATVO's Eurobus runs between Treviso airport and Piazzale Roma, connecting with most flights. Alternatively, the

Where's the boat/bus for…?	**Dove si prende il vaporetto/ l'autobus per…?**
I want a ticket to…	**Desidero uno biglietto per…**
Could you please take these bags to the bus/train/taxi	**Mi porti queste valige fino all'autobus/al treno/al taxi, per favore**
What time does the train/bus leave for the city centre?	**A che ora parte il treno/pullman per il centro?**

No. 6 bus runs from the airport to Treviso's train station, where regular services take 30 min to reach Santa Lucia station in central Venice.

B

BUDGETING FOR YOUR TRIP

To give an idea of what to expect costwise, here is a list of approximate prices in *euros* (€). Note that services marked with an asterisk are fixed by the Venetian authorities; check these in the latest edition of *Un Ospite di Venezia (see page 118)*.

Airport transfer. *By road*: public bus (ACTV) €1; airport bus (ATVO) €3; taxi €35 (up to four people). *By water*: Alilaguna public water launch €10 per person; private water taxi approximately €90 for four people and luggage.

Entertainment. Casino €5 admission. A concert in a main church costs around €25; Fenice opera tickets from €80.

Gondolas. The official daytime rate is €73 for 50 minutes (up to six people), then €37 for each subsequent 25 (read 20) minutes. The evening rate (from 8pm–8am) is €91. Serenaded gondola tours (40 min) are €35 per person.

Guided tours. For a walking tour, allow €25. A boat tour on the *Burchiello* to Padua costs €67 (€24 extra for lunch).

Food. *Tramezzini* (half sandwiches, available at counters in cafés and bars) €1.50; *chichetti* (hot and cold *hors d'oeuvres* at wine bars) from €2 per item; full meal for one at an inexpensive restaurant €20–5; at a moderate restaurant, including cover and service (excluding drinks) €30–40; pizza €6–10; beer €2–5; glass of house wine from €2.

Hotel. For bed and breakfast per night in high season, inclusive of tax: deluxe, €400 and above; expensive, €250–400; moderate, €130–250; inexpensive, under €130.

Lido beach. Entrance to the beach of the Hotel Des Bains €11; beach cabins up to €100 per day.

Museums and attractions. €1.50–7. A museum pass for all civic museums costs €15.50.

Porters. One piece of luggage costs €15.49, two pieces, €20.66.

Public Transport. *Vaporetto*: single fare €3.50, Grand Canal €5, 24-hour ticket €10.50, 72-hour ticket €22.

C

CLIMATE

Winters are cold, summers are hot, and the rest of the year is somewhere in between. The winds off the Adriatic and occasional flooding mean that Venice can be damp and chilly, although very atmospheric, between November and March. June, July and August can be stifling – air-conditioning is essential for a good night's rest at this time of year.

		J	F	M	A	M	J	J	A	S	O	N	D
Max °F		42	46	54	63	71	77	83	83	79	65	54	46
	°C	6	8	12	17	22	25	28	28	26	18	12	8
Min °F		34	34	41	51	57	64	68	66	62	52	43	37
	°C	1	1	5	10	14	18	20	19	17	11	6	3

CLOTHING

A pair of comfortable walking shoes is essential – despite Venice's excellent canal transport network, if you want to sightsee, you'll probably spend most of your time on foot. For summer, pack thin cotton clothing and a light jacket for breezy evening *vaporetto* rides. Remember that when visiting churches you won't be allowed in if your back and shoulders are uncovered or if your shorts go above the knee. For winter trips, take lots of layers, including a warm coat. Some of the better hotels loan out knee boots in case of light flooding but it's a good idea to bring waterproof footwear with you anyway.

Venice is generally an informal city, but stylish dress is appropriate at its smarter restaurants. Men must wear a jacket and tie to gain entry to the Casino.

CRIME AND SAFETY (See also EMERGENCIES and POLICE)

Although Venice is one of the safest cities in Italy, pickpockets and purse-snatchers are not uncommon, and tourists are favourite targets. Carry with you only what is absolutely necessary; leave passports, airline tickets and all but one credit card in the hotel safe. Use a money belt or carry your valuables in an inside pocket. For women, a small purse with strings, worn strapped across the body or under a coat in winter, is best. Be careful on crowded public transport, especially when getting on and off the *vaporetti*, in the crush around San Marco and in deserted streets.

Make photocopies of your airline tickets, driving licence, passport, and other vital documents to facilitate reporting any theft and obtaining replacements. Report thefts to the police, so that you have a statement to file with your insurance claim.

Women should avoid dark, out-of-the-way places, although any danger is usually in terms of being hassled, not in being attacked.

I want to report a theft	**Voglio denunciare un furto**

CUSTOMS AND ENTRY REQUIREMENTS

For citizens of EU countries, a valid passport or identity card is all that is needed to enter Italy for stays of up to 90 days. Citizens of Australia, Canada, New Zealand and the US require only a valid passport. **Visas** (*permesso di soggiorno*). For stays of more than 90 days a visa or residence permit is required. Regulations change from time

I've nothing to declare	**Non ho nulla da dichiarare**

to time, so check with the Italian Embassy in your home country
before you travel.

Customs. Free exchange of non-duty-free goods for personal use is
allowed between countries within the EU. Refer to your home
country's regulating organisation for a current complete list of
import restrictions.

Currency restrictions. Tourists may bring an unlimited amount of
Italian or foreign currency into the country.

D

DISABLED TRAVELLERS

Although the narrow alleys and numerous stepped bridges make
the city tricky for disabled travellers there are ways and means of
getting around and seeing at least some of the major sights. The
larger *vaporetti* (such as numbers 1 and 82) have access for wheelchairs, but the slimmer *motoscafi* should be avoided.

If you understand Italian, the **Informahandicap** organisation
has a useful website at <www.comune.venezia.it/handicap> and
a branch at Ca'Farsetti, Riva del Carbon, San Marco 4136, tel:
041-2718144. Local APT offices *(see page 126)* supply maps
marking the handful of bridges with ramps for wheelchairs and
the keys which operate them. The APT *Where to Stay* booklet indicates which hotels are suitable or partially suitable for disabled
people. The registered charity **Tripscope**, based in the UK (tel:
0845 7585641 or +44 117 939 7782 from outside the UK, <www.
tripscope.org.uk>) offers free help to disabled people planning a
trip abroad.

Accessible attractions (note, however, that no differentiation is
made between full and partial access) include the Basilica di San
Marco, Palazzo Ducale, Ca' Rezzonico, the churches of the Frari,
La Salute, San Zanipolo and San Giorgio Maggiore, Museo Correr
and some other museums.

DRIVING

Venice is a **traffic-free zone**, and the closest you can get to the centre in a car is Piazzale Roma, where there are two large multi-storey car parks. There is also a huge multi-level car park is on the adjacent 'car-park' island of Tronchetto, also the terminal for the car ferry to the Lido, where driving is allowed. There are also two car parks on the mainland at Mestre San Giuliano and Fusina, both of which have easy access to Venice by bus.

Although the outdoor car parks are guarded night and day, it's sensible not to leave anything of value in your car.

Can I park here?	**Posso parcheggiare qui?**

E

ELECTRICITY

A 220-volt current is supplied to all but the oldest of Venice's areas. Bring a multiple adaptor *(una presa multipla)*, or buy one as required.

What's the voltage, 220 or 110?	**Qual è il voltaggio, 220 (duecento-venti) o 110 (centodieci)?**
I'd like an adaptor/a battery	**Vorrei una presa complementare/ una batteria**

EMBASSIES AND CONSULATES *(Ambasciate, Consolati)*

Most consulates can provide lists of English-speaking doctors, lawyers and interpreters.

Australia (Embassy): Via Antonio Bosio 5, 215, Rome;
tel: 06-852721, <www.italy.embassy.gov.au>.
Canada (Consulate): Riviera Ruzzante 25, Padua;
tel: 049-8781147.

Republic of Ireland (Embassy): Piazza di Campetelli 3, Rome;
tel: 06-6979121.
New Zealand (Embassy): Via Zara 28, Rome; tel: 06-4417171.
South Africa (Consulate): Santa Croce 464, Piazzale Roma;
tel: 041-5241599.
UK (Consulate): Piazza Donatori di Sangue 2, Mestre;
tel: 041-5055990.
US (Consulate): Largo Donegani 1, Milan; tel: 02-290351.

EMERGENCIES

In case of an emergency, telephone:
Police **112**
Carabinieri **113** (for urgent police action)
Fire **115**
Ambulance **118**

Careful!	**Attenzione!**	Fire!	**Incendio!**
Help (police)!	**Polizia!**	Stop!	**Stop!**
Stop! Thief!	**Al ladro!**		

G

GETTING THERE

A reliable travel agent will have full details of all the latest flight possibilities, fares and regulations. Alternatively, do your own search on the Internet *(see page 127)*. For airport information, *see page 106*.
By air. Alitalia (from the UK, tel: 0870 544 8259; from the States, tel: 800 223 5730; <www.alitalia.com>) is the main Italian agent for flights to Venice. Within Europe, they operate between Venice and London, Dublin, Brussels, Paris and Barcelona. Other companies flying to Venice from the UK include British Airways (tel: 0870 850 9850, <www.british airways.com>) who operate two flights a day from Gatwick.

Among the low-cost airlines serving Venice are easyJet (tel: 0870 600 000, <www.easyjet.com>) which operates flights from London Gatwick to Marco Polo, Venice; Ryanair (<www.ryanair.com>) run flights from Stansted to Treviso airport (20 miles from Venice). There are also summer charters on offer to travellers from Gatwick, Manchester, Birmingham and other regional airports. Aer Lingus (tel: 0870 876 5000, <www.aerlingus.com>) operates services from Dublin to Venice.

From the US there are direct flights to Venice from New York (Delta Airlines, <www.delta.com>) and from Philadelphia (US Airways, <www.usairways.com>). Alitalia operates regular flights from New York, Boston, Miami, Chicago and Los Angeles to Milan and Rome, with onward connections to Venice. From Australia and New Zealand, flights are generally to Rome, with onward connections possible from there.

Within Italy there are direct flights to Venice from Milan, Naples, Rome and Palermo.

By train. Venice is very well connected by train. Its main station is Stazione Venezia–Santa Lucia (info. tel: 8488-88088). Travel time to Milan is 3 hours, to Florence 3 hours and to Rome 4½ hours.

InterRail cards are valid in Italy, as is the **Eurailpass** for non-European residents (buy yours before you leave home). The **Eurodomino Pass** offers travel on any 3–8 day period in one month in several European countries. Contact Rail Europe, 178 Piccadilly, London W1V 0AL (<www.raileurope.co.uk>). The Trenitalia Pass covering all trains in Italy is valid for unlimited travel for 4–10 days within a two month period. A Trenitalia Saver Pass for the same period offers a discount for 2–5 people travelling together. Travel on Eurostar Italia, Intercity Plus and other high-speed trains is permitted on payment of a supplement.

By bus. Buses from within Italy arrive in Venice at Piazzale Roma. There is a good, cheap bus service between Venice and nearby Padua.

By car. If you travel by car, you will need a current driving licence (with an Italian translation unless it is the standard EU licence) and valid insurance (green card). Additional insurance cover, including a 'return-home' service, is offered by groups including the British and American Automobile Associations. The Channel Tunnel and Cross-Channel car ferries link the UK with France, Belgium and Holland. Once on the continent, you can put your car on a train to Milan (starting points include Boulogne and Paris) and from there you can travel to Venice. Having a car won't help you once you reach Venice, however, as they are not allowed in the centre and must be left in a car park *(see page 112)*.

GUIDES AND TOURS

The tourist office *(see pages 125–6)* can supply you with a list of qualified tour guides if you want a personal tour of a particular site or on a specialist aspect of Venice. All year round there are standard tours (book through hotels and travel agencies), including a two-hour **walking tour** of San Marco, taking in the Basilica, the Palazzo Ducale and a glass-blowing workshop; a two-hour **walking and gondola tour** covering the Frari and the Grand Canal; a one-hour evening **gondola serenade** tour; and a three-hour **islands tour**. It usually costs more to go on an organised tour than to visit the same places independently.

A **cruise** along the Brenta Canal to Padua, aboard the 200-seater *Burchiello* motorboat, makes an interesting (although expensive) day out; book through local travel agencies and hotels. The return journey to Venice is by coach.

CHORUS (tel: 041-27504622, <www.chorusvenezia.org>), a programme that promotes the preservation of the city's churches, offers guided tours from March–June and September–December to a number of churches. A discount pass (€9) is also offered by this group – valid for entrance to 15 churches, the pass may be purchased at any of the participating churches. Free tours are given of the Basilica in summer, while a 'Secret Tour' *(Itinerari Segreti)* shows you the ins and outs of life at the Palazzo Ducale *(see page 36)*.

Evening lectures on the **art and history** of Venice are held during the summer months. Ask at the tourist office for details. For more information on guided tours consult <www.tours-italy.com>.

H

HEALTH AND MEDICAL CARE

If your private health insurance policy does not cover you while abroad (note that Medicare does not have coverage outside the US), take out a short-term policy before leaving home. EU residents should obtain the European Health Insurance Card, available from post offices or online. which entitles them to emergency medical and hospital treatment.

Ask at your hotel if you need a doctor (or dentist) who speaks English. The US and British consulates *(see pages 112–13)* have lists of English-speaking doctors. Many doctors at Venice's main hospital *(ospedale),* next to San Zanipolo church, speak English; for the casualty department *(pronto soccorso),* where medical emergencies are handled, tel: 041-5294516.

Mosquitoes can be a nuisance in Venice in summer, so it's a good idea to take along a small plug-in machine that burns a tablet emitting fumes that are noxious to them. Airport shops sell these, and some hotels also provide them. Take cream with you to soothe bites.

Pharmacies. Italian *farmacias* open during shopping hours and in turn for night and holiday service; the address of the nearest open pharmacy is posted on all pharmacy doors. You can also check the list in *Un Ospite di Venezia (see page 118)* or consult the local press.

I need a doctor/dentist	**Ho bisogno di un medico/dentista**
I've a pain here	**Ho un dolore qui**
a stomach ache	**il mal di stomaco**
a fever	**la febbre**

L

LANGUAGE

All Venetian hotels above a basic standard will have staff who speak some English, French or German and, unless you go well off the beaten track, you should have no problem communicating in shops or restaurants. However, in bars and cafés away from Piazza San Marco, you'll almost certainly have the chance to practise your Italian, and the locals will think more of you for making an effort.

Venetians have a strong dialect, though to the visitor unfamiliar with the Italian language this is academic. However, some terms are useful to know: there is only one *piazza* in Venice – San Marco; other squares are usually called *campo*, although a small square may be known as a *piazzetta*; the term *calle* is used to refer to most streets, but a *salizzada* is a main street, and a covered passage is a *sottoportego*. A *ponte* is a bridge, a canal is a *rio*, and the broad paved walkway along a major waterfront or *canale* is a *riva* or a *fondamenta*.

Notice that both Venetian and Italian names are used in street signs and on maps: for example, San Giuliano is 'San Zulian' and Santi Giovanni e Paolo is 'San Zanipolo' (Giovanni becomes 'Zani').

In Italian the letter 'c' is pronounced 'ch' (as in church) when it is followed by 'e' or 'i,' while 'ch' is a hard sound, like the 'c' in cat.

LOST PROPERTY *(Oggetti Rinvenuti)*

The lost property office, *Ufficio Oggetti Rinvenuti*, is located at Ca' Loredan on Riva del Carbon, 4136 San Marco, near the Rialto Bridge (tel: 041-2748225; open Mon–Fri 8.30am–12.30pm and Mon, Thur 2.30pm–4.30pm). If you lose something on a *vaporetto*, go to the lost property office (open daily 9am–8pm) in the ACTV building at Piazzale Roma. There are also lost property offices at the airport and railway station.

M

MAPS

APT offices *(see page 126)* sell the *Venezia e Isote* map and *Easy-guide* accompanying booklet (€2.50 for the package). This is useful for locating sights and landing stages, but if you want something more detailed, look in any bookstore. For those who plan to stay in Venice any length of time, a worthwhile investment is *Calli, Campielli e Canali*, a volume of very detailed street maps of Venice and its lagoon.

MEDIA

Newspapers and magazines *(giornali, riviste)*. You can find both American and British English-language newspapers at airports and in most city-centre news-stands *(edicola)*; some are available on the day of publication, others with a delay of 24 hours.

Radio and TV *(radio, televisione)*. The Italian state TV network, the RAI *(Radio Televisione Italiana)*, broadcasts three TV channels, which compete with six independent ones. All programmes are in Italian, including British and American feature films and imports, which are dubbed. Most hotels have cable connections for CNN Europe, CNBC and other channels that offer world news in English including BBC World and Sky. The airwaves are crammed with radio stations, most of them broadcasting popular music. The BBC World Service can be picked up on short wave radio.

Venice's free listings magazine *Un Ospite di Venezia* comes out fortnightly and is available in many hotels. It details visitor attractions, events and exhibitions, including opening times and prices, and also has a useful section on practical information. Look out

Do you have English-language newspapers?	**Avete giornali in inglese?**

also for the *LEO Venice Magazine*, featuring articles on culture and news. It comes into a useful pull-out section with practical information on the city. The magazine is also available online at <www.turismovenezia.it/leo>.

MONEY

Currency. Italy's monetary unit is the euro (abbreviated €), which is divided into 100 cents. Banknotes are available in denominations of 500, 200, 100, 50, 20, 10 and 5 euros. There are coins for 2 and 1 euros, and for 50, 20, 10, 5, 2 and 1 cents.

Currency exchange. Currency exchange offices *(cambio)* are usually open Monday to Friday (hours vary, some open all day); some stay open on Saturday. Both *cambio* and banks charge a commission. Banks generally offer higher exchange rates and lower commissions. Passports are sometimes required when changing money.

ATMs. Automatic currency-exchange machines *(bancomat)* are operated by most banks. Independent (non-bank related) ATMs can also be found in the centre of town.

Credit cards and travellers cheques. Most hotels, shops and restaurants take credit cards. If the card's sign is posted in the window of a business, they must accept it; however, some may try to avoid doing so. Travellers cheques are accepted almost everywhere, but you will usually get better value if you exchange them at a bank. Passports are required when cashing travellers cheques.

OPENING HOURS

Banks. Hours are Monday to Friday 8.30am–1.30pm, 2.35–3.35pm.

Bars and restaurants. Some café-bars open for breakfast, but others do not open until around noon; the vast majority shut early, at around 10.30 or 11pm. Nearly all restaurants close for at least one day per week, and some close for parts of August, January and February.

Churches. The 15 CHORUS churches *(see page 115)* are open Monday to Saturday 10am–5pm, Sunday 1–5pm. Other churches are normally open Monday to Saturday from around 8am until noon and from 3 or 4pm until 6 or 7pm. Sunday openings vary, some are only open for morning services.

Museums and galleries. Most close on one day of the week, usually Monday, and are otherwise open from 9 or 10am until 6pm.

Shops. Business hours are Monday to Saturday, 9 or 10am until 1pm, and 3 or 4pm until 7pm. Some shops are open all day and even on Sundays, particularly in peak season.

P

POLICE *(Polizia, Carabinieri.* See also EMERGENCIES)

Although you rarely see or need them Venice's police function efficiently and are courteous. The emergency police telephone number is **112** or **113**, which will put you through to a switchboard and someone who speaks your language. Serious matters are handled by the *carabinieri*.

Where's the nearest police station?	**Dov'è il più vicino posto di polizia?**

POST OFFICES *(Posta, Ufficio Postale)*

The main office (open Mon–Sat 8.30am–6.30pm) is inside the Fondachi dei Tedeschi at the Rialto, while the two main sub-offices (both open Mon–Fri 8.30am–2pm, Sat 8.30am–1pm) are on the Zattere (Dorsoduro) and Calle dell'Ascensione, just off Piazza San Marco. The lobby of the main office can be used 24 hours a day for faxes and express and registered letters.

Postage stamps *(francobolli)* are also sold at tobacconists *(tabacchi)*, marked by a distinctive 'T' sign.

| I'd like a stamp for this letter/postcard | **Desidero un francobollo per questa lettera/cartolina** |

PUBLIC HOLIDAYS *(Giorni Festivi)*

Banks, government offices and most shops and museums close on public holidays. When a major holiday falls on a Thursday or a Tuesday, Italians may make a *ponte* (bridge) to the weekend, meaning that Friday or Monday is taken, too.

The most important holidays are:

1 January	**Capodanno or Primo dell'Anno**	New Year's Day
6 January	**Epifania**	Epiphany
25 April	**Festa della Liberazione**	Liberation Day
1 May	**Festa del Lavoro**	Labour Day
25 August	**Ferragosto**	Assumption Day
1 November	**Ognissanti**	All Saints' Day
8 December	**Immacolata Concezione**	Immaculate Conception
25 December	**Natale**	Christmas Day
26 December	**Santo Stefano**	St Stephen's Day
Movable date	**Lunedi di Pasqua**	Easter Monday

The **Festa della Salute** on 21 November is a special Venetian holiday, when many shops close.

PUBLIC TRANSPORT

Waterbuses *(Vaporetti)*. The only public transport in Venice is water-borne, and an efficient *vaporetto* will take you to within a short walk of anywhere you want to get to. Venice is so compact, however, that for short journeys, it is often quicker to walk. *Vaporetti* ply the Grand Canal, go round to the north shore of the city (where the main stop is Fondamente Nuove) and shuttle to and from the minor islands. They run 24 hours a day and provide a wonderful perspective on the city. A schedule for all *vaporetti* lines may be obtained from the Centro Informazioni ACTV at Piazzale Roma; tel: 041-2424; <www.actv.it>.

It's best to buy your ticket in advance from the ticket offices that are on, or close to, the landing stages at the main stops, or at any shop displaying an ACTV sign. At the time of press, the individual fare was €3.50, or €5 for a Grand Canal ticket (this is valid for 90 minutes and more than one trip is allowed). However, you can buy one-, three- and seven-day passes as well as family or group fares. A 24-hour or 72-hour pass is a good investment if you intend seeing much of the city (or if you want to use the *vaporetti* simply to hop across the Grand Canal). If you haven't bought a ticket before boarding, you can purchase one on board from the conductor for a small surcharge. Remember to validate your ticket by stamping it at the machine on the landing stage or you'll have to pay a surcharge.

The main services are: No. 1 *(accelerato)*, which stops at every stage along the Grand Canal; No. 82 *(diretto)*, which goes direct from Piazzale Roma to San Marco and the Lido; and LN (Laguna Nord), which runs from Fondamente Nuove to the islands of Murano, Burano and Torcello.

Nos 41 and 42 describe Venice in a clockwise, circular route, calling at San Zaccaria, the Redentore (Palladio's masterpiece), Piazzale Roma, Ferrovia (the railway station), Fondamente Nuove, San Michele and Murano, before returning to San Zaccaria, via San Pietro. *Vaporetti* 51 and 52 provide long, scenic, circular tours around the periphery of Venice, as well as stopping at Murano; in summer they also go on to the Lido (you may need to change at Fondamente Nuove to do the whole route).

Note that the circular routes no longer serve the Arsenale, travelling instead up the Cannaregio Canal, stopping at Guglie, and then skirting the northern shores of Venice, including Fondamente Nuove and Madonna dell'Orto (get off at the Orto stop for Tintoretto's church), the shipyards (Bacini stop), San Pietro di Castello and, eventually, the Lido.

Traghetti. The *traghetto* (ferry) service operates at various points across the Grand Canal. It is customary (but not obligatory) to stand while crossing. The cost of using the *traghetto* is €0.40.

Water taxis. If you need a door-to-door service (or you want to avoid the crowds), ask your hotel to call a *motoscafo*. Although fast, they are extremely expensive.

When's the next *vaporetto* for…?	**A che ore parte il prossimo vaporetto per…?**
What's the fare to...?	**Quanto costa il biglietto per...?**
I want a ticket to...	**Vorrei un biglietto per...**

R

RELIGION

Although predominantly Roman Catholic, Venice has congregations of all the major religions *(see list below)*. Check *Un Ospite di Venezia (see page 118)* or ask at your hotel or the local tourist office for details.

Anglican. Church of St George, Campo San Vio, Dorsoduro.

Evangelical Lutheran. Campo Santi Apostoli, Cannaregio.

Evangelical Waldensian/Methodist. Santa Maria Formosa, Castello.

Greek Orthodox. Ponte dei Greci, Castello.

Jewish Synagogue. Campo del Ghetto Vecchio 1149, Cannaregio (tel: 041-715012 or enquire at the Jewish Community Centre, Campo del Ghetto Nuovo).

Roman Catholic. Basilico di San Marco. Masses in Italian; confession in several languages throughout the summer.

T

TELEPHONES *(Telefoni)*

The country code for Italy is 39, and the area code for the city of Venice is 041. Note that you must dial the '041' prefix even when making local calls within the city of Venice.

Telecom Italia public phones, which can be used for long distance and international calls, can be found all over the city. For these you need phone cards *(schede telefoniche)* which are sold in tobacconists and post offices in denominations of €2.50, €5 and €7.50. Some public phones also take major credit cards. There are also pre-paid international phone cards – for these you need to dial a toll-free number found on the back of the card. To make an international call, dial 00, followed by the country code (Australia +61, Ireland +353, New Zealand +64, South Africa +27, UK +44, US & Canada +1), then the area code (often minus the initial zero) and finally the individual number.

You must insert a coin or a card to access a dial tone even when making a toll-free call. Be aware of exorbitant hotel charges for direct calls and service charges for toll-free calls on their phone lines.

TIME ZONES

Italy follows Central European Time (GMT+1) and from late March to late September clocks are put one hour ahead (GMT+2). The following chart indicates time differences during the summer:

New York	London	**Italy**	Jo'burg	Sydney	Auckland
6am	11am	**noon**	noon	8pm	10pm

TIPPING

A service charge of around 10 or 15 percent is usually added to restaurant bills, so it is not necessary to tip very much – perhaps just round the bill up slightly. However, it is normal practice to tip bellboys, tour guides and the elderly gondolier posted at the landing station who helps you into and out of your craft.

Tip others as follows: Hotel porter €1.50 per bag; hotel maid €1–2 per day.

Keep the change.	**Tenga il resto**.

TOILETS (*Toilette, Gambinetto*)

There are public toilets (usually of a reasonable standard but with a charge) in the airport, railway station, car parks, museums, galleries and in many squares in the city. You can also use the facilities in restaurants, bars and cafés but only if you order a drink of some sort. Note that *signori* means men; *signore* means women.

Where are the toilets?	**Dove sono i gabinetti?**

TOURIST INFORMATION

The **Italian National Tourist Board** (ENIT) has a website at <www.enit.it>. Offices abroad can provide basic tourist information, lists of accommodation, etc, in advance of your trip.

Australia Level 26, 44 Market Street, Sydney; tel: 02-9262 1666.

Canada 175 Bloor Street East, Suite 907, South Tower, Toronto, Ontario M4W 3RB; tel: 416-925 4882; <www.italiantourism.com>.

UK/Ireland 1 Princes Street, London W1B 2AY; tel: 020-7408 1254; <www.italiantouristboard.co.uk>.

US

• **Chicago**: 500 N Michigan Avenue, Suite 2240, Chicago, IL 60611; tel: 312-644 0996; <www.italiantourism.com>.

• **Los Angeles**: 12400 Wilshire Boulevard, Suite 550, Los Angeles CA 90025; tel: 310-820-1898; <www.italiantourism.com>.

• **New York**: 630 Fifth Avenue, Suite 1565, New York, NY 10111; tel: 212-245 4822; <www.italiantourism.com>.

Tourist Information Offices in Venice. The main office is on the western corner of Piazza San Marco and offers both general information and booking for some tours and events: APT Venezia, San Marco 71/f, Calle dell'Ascensione/Procuratie Nuove, tel: 041-5298711; fax: 041-5230399; open daily 9am–3.30pm. An equally convenient but less busy office is on the St Mark's waterfront, in a pavilion beside the public gardens. It also has a good Venice-themed bookshop: APT Venezia, Ex-Giardini-Reali (tel: as above; daily 10am–6pm). The tourist office at the railway station is also handy: APT Venezia, Ferrovia Santa Lucia (daily 8am–6.30pm), as is the one at the airoprt: APT Marco Polo (daily 9.30am–7.30pm). This mostly deals with accommodation and transport tickets. To contact the central tourist office e-mail: <info@turismovenezia.it>; <www.turismovenezia.it> (events, itineraries, excursions, hotels and advice).

Rolling Venice. If you or someone in your party is aged between 14 and 29, enrol with the official youth-oriented discount scheme known as 'Rolling Venice'. For around €3, you are entitled to discounts for 25 museums and galleries, 72-hour *vaporetto* tickets, as well as shopping, restaurant and hotel discounts. You also receive a free guide booklet containing details of interesting walking itineraries. Enrol at the railway station, the ACTV office in Piazzale Roma or any of the APT (tourist) offices.

Venice Card. This innovation, aimed at tourists, comes in two colours: **blue**, offering unlimited access to local public transport services and toilets, and **orange**, which also offers access to municipal museums, including the Palazzo Ducale. Both cards also entitle you to discounts on some hotels, hostels, restaurants and shops. Cards can be bought for 1, 3 or 7 days. The cheapest way to buy the card is to book online at <www.venicecard.com> 48 hours in advance. You will be issued with a voucher which can be exchanged for the card at one of the VELA offices (Piazzale Roma, Santa Lucia railway station, Tronchetto car park or Marco Polo airport). Alternatively you can reserve a card by phoning the call centre (tel +39 041 2424 from abroad) and obtaining a code-number which can be exchanged for the card at a VELA office. The price structure is quite complex and depends on age and length of stay.

W

WEBSITES

For on-line sites that will help you to plan your trip to Venice, the following are good places to start: <www.turismovenezia.it>, the website of the local tourist board, and <www.meetingvenice .it>, the site of the Regional Tourist Board, which offers information on hotels, events, restaurants and up-to-date museum opening times. The City Council's site, <www.comune.venezia.it>, has many useful links.

   Other sites with information about hotels, events and things to do are <www.veneziasi.it>, <www.initaly.com> and <www.venice online.it>. For waterbus maps and timetables consult <www.actv.it>.
Internet cafés. Venice has a cluster of internet cafes, including Net House Internet Café (Campo Santo Stefano) and Libreria Mondadori (San Marco).

Y

YOUTH HOSTELS *(Ostelli della Gioventù)*

There are five youth hostels in Venice,with three in Giudecca, the best location. Particularly recommended: **Ex Junghans** (Giudecca 394, tel: 041-5210801) and **Ostello Venezia** (Fondamenta delle Zitelle, Giudecca 86; tel: 041-5238211; <www.ostellionline.org>).

Recommended Hotels

Venice is nearly always busy with tourists, so book your hotel early, particularly in high season (spring to early autumn, around Christmas week and during Carnival). The following is a just a selection of the many hotels in the city, organised by area. In general, the closer to San Marco, the more expensive a hotel will be. The ranges below indicate the price of a double room with bath or shower per night, including breakfast and tax, during high season. Except where noted, all major credit cards are accepted. Note that the nearest *vaporetto* stop to a hotel is given at the end of each listing. For further information on accommodation in Venice, *see page 105*.

€€€€	€400 and above
€€€	€250–400
€€	€180–250
€	€180 and under

SAN MARCO, CASTELLO AND CANNAREGIO

Ai Do Mori € *Calle Larga San Marco 658, tel: 041-5289293, fax: 041-5205328, <www.hotelaidomori.com>*. Climb three flights to get to this tidy 11-roomed hotel just steps from the Basilica. It has small, renovated rooms, all with air-conditioning and private bathrooms. Rooms on the upper floors have views of the domes of San Marco; the attic-level 'Painter's Room' (reserve months ahead) has a private deck and great vista. Excellent staff. No breakfast. ACTV: San Zaccaria.

Bel Sito & Berlino €–€€ *Campo Santa Maria del Giglio, San Marco 2517, tel: 041-5223365, fax: 041-5204083, e-mail: <info@ hotelbelsito.info>, <www.hotelbelsito.info>*. This friendly hotel, in a great location between Piazza San Marco and Accademia Bridge, has 34 bedrooms furnished in pleasant, traditional style. Rooms at the front overlook a lavish Baroque church; the ones at the rear of the hotel are quieter. Wheelchair access. ACTV: Santa Maria del Giglio.

Bernardi–Semanzato € *Cannaregio 4363, tel: 041-5227257, fax: 041-5222424, e-mail:* <*info@hotelbernardi.com*>, <*www.hotel bernardi.com*>. This hotel, situated in Cannaregio, just across the canal from the San Marco district, has helpful staff and 14 plain but modern rooms, 12 with private bathrooms. ACTV: Ca' D'Oro.

Bisanzio €€–€€€ *Calle della Pietà, Castello 3651, tel: 041-5203100, fax: 041-5204114,* <*www.bisanzio.com*>. In a peaceful spot just off the Riva degli Schiavoni, the Bisanzio has 47 simply furnished traditional rooms, a courtyard and terraces. ACTV: San Zaccaria.

Campiello €€ *Riva degli Schiavoni, San Zaccaria, Castello, 4647, tel: 041-5205764, fax: 041-5205798,* <*www.hcampiello.it*>. A well-run, family-owned hotel located just off the Riva degli Schiavoni with cosy public areas and 16 traditional rooms. ACTV: San Zaccaria.

Casa Verardo €€–€€€ *Camp SS Filippo e Giacomo, Castello 4765, tel: 041-5286127, fax: 041-5232765, email:* <*info@casaverardo.it*>, <*www.casaverardo.it*>. This intimate, family-run hotel in a small, renovated 16th-century palace is extremely central (around 200m/yds from Piazza San Marco), despite being tucked away and quite tricky to find. Traditional, spacious rooms. ACTV: San Zaccaria.

Castello €€ *Calle della Sacrestia, off Campo Santi Filippo e Giacomo, Castello 4365; tel: 041-5230217, fax: 041-5211023, email:* <*info@hotelcastello.it*> <*www.hotelcastello.it*>. The Castello is a small, cosy hotel next to a lively square. The rooms are all modern, and some are decorated with traditional touches. ACTV: San Zaccaria.

Colombina €€€ *Calle de Remedio, Castello 4416, tel: 041-5288631, fax: 041-2419150,* <*www.hotelcolombina.com*>. This lovely hotel, which opened in 1999, is housed in a canalside *palazzo* overlooking the Bridge of Sighs. It has 33 tastefully decorated rooms with all amenities. Two quaint top-floor rooms have roof decks with wonderful views of San Marco. Wheelchair access. ACTV: San Zaccaria.

Danieli €€€€+ *Riva degli Schiavoni, Castello 4196, tel: 041-5226480, fax: 041-5200208,* <*www.starwood.com*>. The most dramatic of Venice's luxury hotels, situated beside the Palazzo Ducale, the Danieli has sumptuous neo-Gothic public areas set around a balconied staircase, a rooftop restaurant with sweeping vistas, and suites furnished with antiques. Note that the majority of doubles are in newer wings. The hotel has private beach facilities at the Lido. Wheelchair access. ACTV: San Zaccaria.

Flora €€ *Calle della Pergola, off Calle Larga XXII Marzo, San Marco 2283/A; tel: 041-5205844, fax: 041-5228217, <www.hotel flora.it>*. Family-run Flora is in a great location and has 44 tradition-ally decorated rooms which vary in size. It has attractive public areas, a secluded little garden and wheelchair access. ACTV: Vallaresso.

Gabrielli Sandwirth €€€€ *Riva degli Schiavoni, Castello 4110, tel: 041-5231580, fax: 041-5209455*. Set in a Gothic palace, with great vistas from its rooftop sun terrace, this large hotel has rooms with pleasant, traditional decor and 1960s-style public areas, which are rather in need of updating. In summer meals are served in a pretty courtyard. Also has a private garden. ACTV: San Zaccaria or Arsenale.

Giorgione €€€ *SS Apolstoli, Cannaregio 4587, tel: 041-5225810, fax: 041-5239092, <www.hotelgiorgione.com>*. This is a delightful hotel with 70 comfortable, renovated rooms. The fact that there are no water views, and that it is in Cannaregio, make it comparatively well priced for its class. The nicest rooms are the doubles with tiny private roof decks and the terrace suites. ACTV: Ca' d'Oro.

Grand Hotel dei Dogi €€€–€€€€ *Fondamenta Madonna dell' Orto, Cannaregio 3500, tel: 041-2208111, fax: 041-722278, email: <reservation.online@boscolo.com>, <www.boscolohotels.it>*. The 18th-century Palazzo Rizzo Patarol, previously the seat of the French and Savoy embassies, has been converted into a 5-star hotel. Advan-tages over the more central hotels are the extensive gardens leading down to the lagoon and a peaceful setting in the pretty Madonna dell' Orto neighbour. Hourly water shuttle to the centre. ACTV: Orto.

Gritti Palace €€€€+ *Campo Santa Maria del Giglio, San Marco 2467; tel: 041-794611, fax: 041-5200942, <www.starwood.com>*. In a 15th-century doge's palace looking out on to the Grand Canal, the Gritti Palace offers the last word in traditional grandeur and personal attention. The 88 rooms are beautiful – many have hand-painted 18th-century decor. Wheelchair access. ACTV: Santa Maria del Giglio.

Hotel Wildner €€ *Riva degli Schiavoni, Castello 4161; tel: 041-5227463, fax: 041-5265615, <www.veneziahotels.com>.* The Wildner is a small, basic but comfortable hotel with a restaurant. Ask for one of the rooms at the front, as these have lovely views across the lagoon. ACTV: San Zaccaria.

Kette €€–€€€ *Piscina San Moisè, San Marco 2053; tel: 041-5207766, fax: 041-5228964, <www.hotelkette.com>.* Located in a beautifully renovated old house with polished wood and warm mellow furnishings extending to the bedrooms, this mid-sized hotel is particularly popular with tour groups. Just a short hop from Piazza San Marco. Wheelchair access. ACTV: Vallaresso.

La Fenice et des Artistes €€ *Campiello della Fenice, San Marco 1936; tel: 041-5232333, fax: 041-5203721, <www.fenicehotels.it>.* This atmospheric 65-roomed hotel located next to the site of the Fenice opera house *(see page 87)* tends to attract visitors interested in the arts; it's popular with musicians too. In one wing, rooms are decorated traditionally, while in the other they are modern and a little bland; most are air-conditioned. Amenities include terraces and a garden. ACTV: Santa Maria del Giglio.

La Residenza €€ *Campo Bandiera e Moro, Castello 3608; tel: 041-5285315, fax: 041-5238859, <www.venicelaresidenza.com>.* An atmospheric 14th-century palace with unusual public areas. Set on a pleasant square, the hotel offers just 15 simple but adequate bedrooms – book ahead to ensure one of the best ones. ACTV: San Zaccaria or Arsenale.

Locanda Leon Bianco €–€€ *Corte del Leon Bianco, Cannaregio 5629, tel: 041-5233572, fax: 041-2416392, email: <info@leonbianco.it>, <www.leonbianco.it>.* This seven-roomed hotel, opened in 1999, is entered through an unprepossessing courtyard and foyer that were once part of a Grand Canal palace. Upstairs, the traditional rooms are very comfortable – three spacious rooms with spectacular canal vistas offer excellent value. ACTV: Ca' d'Oro.

Locanda Novecento €€ *Calle del Dose, San Marco 2683, tel: 041-2413765, fax: 041-5212145, email: <info@novecento.biz>, <www.locandanovecento.it>*. A warm and welcoming little hotel located a few minutes' walk from Piazza San Marco. Opened in 2001, it is owned by the Sore family, as is the Flora *(see page 130)*, but is very different in style. Decor is an imaginative blend of Moroccan, Turkish and oriental styles. There are just nine rooms, all individually furnished. Good buffet breakfasts are served in the pretty little courtyard in summer. ACTV: Santa Maria del Giglio.

Luna Baglioni €€€€ *Calle Vallaresso. Calle de l'Ascension, San Marco 1243; tel: 041-5289840, fax: 041-5287260, <www.baglioni hotels.com>*. This large, heavily modernised hotel beside Piazza San Marco has five-star aspirations and an historic pedigree. The public rooms are splendid, but only a quarter of the traditionally furnished bedrooms have good views. Wheelchair access. ACTV: Vallaresso.

Metropole €€€€ *Riva degli Schiavoni, Castello 4149; tel: 041-5205044, fax: 041-5223679, <www.hotelmetropole.com>*. This restored early-19th-century building facing the lagoon has 64 tasteful rooms, peppered with antiques. Fantastic service. ACTV: San Zaccaria.

Pensione Bucintoro €–€€ *Riva degli Schiavoni, Castello 2135; tel: 041-5223240, fax: 041-523522,. <www.hotelbucintoro.com>*. Although Pensione Bucintoro's 28 bedrooms are simply furnished in modern style, all have splendid views over the lagoon and the quay towards San Giorgio Maggiore. The pleasant breakfast room is a plus point. No credit cards. ACTV: Arsenale.

Rialto €€€ *Riva del Ferro, San Marco 5149; tel: 041-520 9166, fax: 041-5238958, <www.rialtohotel.com>*. This large hotel is situated right beside the Rialto Bridge and has spectacular views along the Grand Canal. Modern decor in the bedrooms. Wheelchair access. ACTV: Rialto.

San Fantin € *Campiello della Fenice, San Marco 1930/A; tel: 041-523 1401, fax: 041-5231401, e-mail: <info@hotelsanfantin.com>, <www.hotelfantin.com>.* This is a tiny, pleasant hotel in a quiet location, near the Fenice, with modest, modern rooms. It closes in winter but opens for Carnevale. ACTV: Santa Maria del Giglio.

San Samuele € *Salizzada San Samuele, San Marco 3358, tel/fax: 041-5228045, email: <info@albergosansamuele.it>, <www.albergo sansamuele.it>* Ten simple rooms, both with and without private bathrooms, in a bright friendly place on a street dominated by trendy galleries. ACTV: San Samuele.

Saturnia & International €€€€ *Via XXII Marzo, San Marco 2399; tel: 041-5208377, fax: 041-5207131, <www.hotelsaturnia.it>.* Built around a 14th-century doge's palace, this large hotel has been run by the same family since 1908. The rooms in the old part are more sumptuous than those in the new section. Wheelchair access. ACTV: San Marco.

Savoia & Jolanda €€€–€€€€ *Riva degli Schiavoni, Castello 4187, tel: 041-5206644, fax: 041-5207494, <www.hotelsavoia jolanda.com>.* This grand-looking establishment has many rooms with balconies opening on to the lagoon. Bedrooms have been decorated in simple modern style; there's an annex with cheaper rooms. Wheelchair access. ACTV: San Zaccaria.

Violino d'Oro €€–€€€ *Campiello Barozzi, San Marco 2001; tel: 041-2770841, fax: 041-2771001, <www.violinodoro.com>.* Just steps from San Marco, this hotel, which opened in 1999, offers 26 tastefully designed rooms. It has a total no-smoking policy. Wheelchair access. ACTV: Vallaresso.

Vivaldi €€€€ *Riva degli Schiavoni, Locanda Vivaldi 4152–3, Castello, tel: 041-2770477, fax: 041-2770489, <www.locandavivaldi. it>.* Another hotel opened in 1999, the Vivaldi is notable for its opulent Baroque-style decor. Its 25 well-appointed rooms are tasteful but varied in appeal: some are spacious, with views of the lagoon, while others are rather small. Wheelchair access. ACTV: San Zaccaria.

Westin Europa & Regina €€€€+ *San Marco 2159, tel: 041-2400001, fax: 041-5231533, <www.westin.com/europaregina>*. This large, renowned Grand Canal hotel has spectacular terrace views over Santa Maria della Salute. There is an excellent canal-front restaurant and beach and recreation facilities at the Lido. Wheelchair access. ACTV: Vallaresso.

SAN POLO AND DORSODURO

Agli Alboretti €€ *Rio Terrà Antonio Foscarini, Dorsoduro 884, tel: 041-5230058, fax: 041-5210158, email: <info@aglialboretti.com>, <www.aglialboretti.com>*. Lovely family-run hotel with nautical-themed decor and quaint rooms. ACTV: Accademia or Zattere.

American €€€ *San Vio, Dorsoduro 628, tel: 041-5204733, fax: 041-5204048, email: <reception@hotelamerican.com>, <www.hotelamerican.com>*. All the rooms of this small, well-run hotel are furnished in tasteful, traditional Venetian style. Pretty canalside setting. actv: Accademia.

Antica Locanda Sturion €€ *Calle del Sturion, San Polo 679; tel: 041-5236243, fax: 041-5228378, <www.locandasturion.com>*. The Locanda Sturion, is on the top floor of an historic building near the Rialto markets, with its breakfast and reading room overlooking the Grand Canal. Elaborate baroque-style decor. 11 rooms. ACTV: Rialto.

Belle Arti €€ *Via Dorsoduro 912/A, tel: 041-5226230, fax: 041-5280043, <www.hotelbellearti.com>*. This mid-sized hotel near the Accademia is located within a modern building with a large court-yard garden. The decor is mostly traditional Venetian. Wheelchair access. ACTV: Accademia or Zattere.

Ca' Pisani €€€ *Rio Terrà Antonio Foscarini 979a, tel: 041 2401411, fax: 041 2771061, email: <info@capisanihotel.it>, <www.capisanihotel.it>*. Venice's first designer hotel, converted from a 16th-century palazzo close to the Accademia. Minimalist decor with stylish Art Deco furnishings and features. Bedrooms come with internet connection and state-of-the-art bathrooms.

Surprisingly good value for a 4-star hotel. Facilities include a bistro/wine bar and a roof-top terrace. ACTV: Accademia.

Messner € *Salute, Dorsoduro 216, tel: 041-5227443, fax: 041-522 7266, email: <messnerinfo@tin.it>, <www.hotelmessner.it>*. Messner is a small, well-run hotel on a quiet street close to the church of Santa Maria della Salute. It has small, comfortable bedrooms and a breakfast terrace. It is one of the more affordable of Venice's hotels, popular with a younger clientele and student groups. ACTV: Salute.

Pensione Accademia Villa Maravege €€€ *Fondamenta Bollani, Dorsoduro 1058, tel: 041-5210188, fax: 041-5239152, <www.pensioneaccademia.it>*. A small, traditional and gorgeous hotel in a 17th-century villa (the setting for the film *Summertime*, starring Katharine Hepburn), with delightful gardens. Excellent location close to the Accademia Gallery. Popular, so book well ahead. ACTV: Accademia.

Pensione La Calcina €€ *Zattere, Dorsodoro 780, tel: 041-5206466, fax: 041-5227045, <www.lacalcina.com>*. Vistas of the Giudecca Canal, fresh renovations and lovely British Victorian decor mark this small hotel where the 19th-century social commentator, art historian and writer John Ruskin (*The Stones of Venice*) once stayed. A library of books on Venice, panoramic roof-deck, two tiny quaint inexpensive singles and an attentive staff are among the pluses. The rooms with private terraces are superb. No TVs. ACTV: Zattere or Accademia.

San Cassiano (Ca' Favretto) €€€ *Calle della Rosa, Santa Croce 2232, tel: 041-5241768, fax: 041-721033, <www.sancassiano.it>*. In an atmospheric 14th-century palace slightly off the beaten track. The 35 rooms are well equipped; the most popular ones are facing the Ca' d'Oro over the canal. Wheelchair access. ACTV: San Stae.

GIUDECCA

Hotel Cipriani €€€€+ *Giudecca 10, tel: 041-5207744, fax: 041-5203930, <www.hotelcipriani.it>*. Arguably Venice's most luxurious hotel, the Cipriani consists of modern buildings set in a lovely garden with a swimming pool, and its 98 rooms have every amenity – those in the 15th-century Palazzo Vendramin annex even come with a butler. Extras include saunas, tennis courts and a hotel launch for shuttling guests to and from San Marco. Wheelchair access. ACTV: Zitelle.

THE LIDO

Hotel Des Bains €€€€ *Lungomare Marconi 17, tel: 041-5265921, fax: 041-5260113, <www.starwood.com/italy>*. Forever associated with Visconti's *Death in Venice* (partly filmed here) and Thomas Mann *(see page 84)*, this grand hotel with a large garden, two tennis courts and a swimming pool is full of Belle Epoque ambience. Faces its private beach on the Lido. Popular with film stars during the Film Festival. 195 rooms. Open April–Oct.

Rigel €€ *Via Enrico Dandolo 13, tel: 041-5268810, fax: 041-2760077*. This friendly little hotel is set in its own garden and situated close to the Piazzale Santa Maria Elisabetta. Open April–Oct.

Westin Excelsior €€€€ *Lungo Marconi 41, tel: 041-5260201, fax: 041-5267276, <www.westin.com>*. The Lido's only 5-star hotel, this beachside Moorish-Gothic fantasy, constructed during the early 1900s, was originally billed as the most glamorous resort hotel in the world. It offers 189 large, modern rooms, seven tennis courts and a swimming pool. There's also a free launch service to Venice. Probably a choice for business travellers or families rather than those wanting the most romantic option. Open April–Oct.

SAN CLEMENTE

San Clemente Palace €€€–€€€€ *Isola di San Clemente 1, tel: 041-2445001, fax: 041-2445800, email: <sanclemente@thi.it>, <www.sanclemente.thi.it>*. One of the cheaper 5-star Venetian hotels, the San Clemente Palace is set on the small island of San Clemente in the southern lagoon. A shuttle service links it to San Marco, just 10 minutes away. In the past San Clemente has variously been a monastery island, military depot, cats' home and lunatic asylum. Today it's a luxury resort with three restaurants (open to non-residents), a swimming pool, bars and extensive grounds.

Recommended Restaurants

Below is a selection of some of Venice's most appealing restaurants, organised by area, with the nearest *vaporetto* stop to each establishment given at the end of its entry. Unless otherwise indicated, all restaurants are open for lunch and dinner.

It's advisable to reserve in high season (spring to early autumn, at Carnival and during Christmas week), for both lunch and dinner, and all year round if a restaurant is especially popular and you want a choice seat. Note that nearly all restaurants close at least one day per week and many also shut during part of late July, August, January and February. Except where noted, all major credit cards are accepted.

To give an idea of the price for a three-course meal for one, including wine, cover and service, we have used the following symbols:

€€€€	€65 and above
€€€	€45–€65
€€	€30–€45
€	€30 and under

SAN MARCO, CASTELLO AND CANNAREGIO

Al Covo €€€–€€€€ *Campiello della Pescheria, Castello 3968, tel: 041-5223812.* This relaxed, cosy restaurant created by chef Cesare Benelli and his Texan wife, Diane, has a worldwide reputation for excellent quality fresh seafood innovatively prepared according to Venetian traditions. During the autumn, duck and game birds are added to the menu. Closed Wed and Thurs. ACTV: San Zaccaria.

Al Graspo de Ua €€€€ *Calle dei Bombaseri, San Marco, tel: 041-5200150.* A lovely old-school *ristorante* serving Venetian cuisine and specialising in seafood. This has become a fashionable place to be seen. Closed Mon. ACTV: Rialto.

Alla Rivetta €€ *Ponte San Provolo, off Campo Santi Filippo e Giacomo, Castello 4625, tel: 041-5287302.* The emphasis in this lively restaurant is on fish dishes, especially with fish-and-pasta combinations, such as gnocchi stuffed with crab. The *tiramisù* and *cichetti* are also second to none. Closed Mon. ACTV: San Zaccaria.

Alle Testiere €€ *Calle del Mondo Novo, Castello 5801, tel: 041-5227220.* A tiny place with a changing daily menu and inventive twists on traditional Venetian cuisine. Great wine list. Reservations essential. Closed Sun and Mon. ACTV: Rialto.

Bistrot de Venise €–€€ *Calle dei Fabbri, San Marco 4685, tel: 041-5236651.* Venetians and visitors alike come for salads at lunch and tried-and-tested recipes at night. A good place for night owls, this bistro stays open until midnight; occasional live music. ACTV: Rialto.

Corte Sconta €€€ *Calle del Pestrin, Castello 3886, tel: 041-5227024.* This hard-to-find rustic restaurant with a garden court-yard has one of the best menus in town, with superb *antipasti* and seafood and outstanding house wine. Closed Sun, Mon, Jan and mid-July to mid-Aug. ACTV: Arsenale.

Da Ivo €€€€ *Ramo dei Fuseri, San Marco 1809, tel: 041-5285004.* Both Venetian and Tuscan cuisines are served here – risotto with cuttlefish ink heads the menu, while Florentine specialities include chicken and T-bone steak. However, the main pull is the atmospheric, intimate dining room. Closed Sun and Jan 6–31. ACTV: Vallaresso.

Da Raffaele €€€ *San Marco 2347 (Ponte delle Ostreghe), tel: 041-5232317.* This restaurant's canalside terrace is ideal for summer meals, and in winter you dine indoors amid medieval surroundings. Grilled meats and seafood are especially recommended. Closed Thurs and Dec 10 to Carnevale. ACTV: Santa Maria del Giglio.

Fiaschetteria Toscana €€€ *Salizzada San Giovanni Crisostomo, Cannaregio 5719, tel: 041-5285281.* Despite its name, Venetian cuisine prevails in this gracious but often crowded family-run restaurant with a garden. Top choices include the excellent fish selection – notably scallops with almonds, cuttlefish or *schie* (tiny shrimps) with polenta – liver *alla veneziana* and great desserts. Closed Tues and lunch on Wed; and July. ACTV: Rialto.

Harry's Bar €€€€+ *Calle Vallaresso San Marco 1323, tel: 041-5285777.* This legendary hotspot is a little unpredictable and has prices to make you weep but on a good day it does heavenly food – it was here that *carpaccio* (thin slices of raw beef) was invented. The *bellini* (prosecco and fresh white peach juice) is also an invention of Harry's, although out of peach season they are best avoided. It's more stylish to dine downstairs at the bar, just as Hemingway once did, rather than sitting in the upstairs room. ACTV: Vallaresso.

La Cusina €€€€ *Hotel Europa e Regina, off Calle Larga XXII Marzo, San Marco 2159; tel: 041-5213785.* A combination of the most dramatic terrace on the Grand Canal and beautifully presented Venetian *haute cuisine* make this a good choice for that special romantic dinner. ACTV: Vallaresso.

Mascareta €€ *Calle Lunga Santa Maria Formosa, Castello 5183, tel: 041-5230744.* A bustling casual place with a young clientele, Mascareta is great for wine and *cichetti* (snacks). No credit cards. Closed Sun. ACTV: Rialto.

Metropole Hotel €€€ *Riva degli Schiavoni, Castello 4149, tel: 041-5205044.* This hotel has an elegant restaurant, which specialises in traditional Venetian cuisine. Garden dining in summer. Reservations necessary. ACTV: San Zaccaria.

Osteria Ai Assassini €–€€ *Rio Terrà degli Assassini 3695, San Marco, tel: 041-5287986.* Lively pub-like place with great soups. Baked fish and seafood dishes are the best choices here; *cappe sante al pomodoro* (scallops with tomato) come highly recommended. Closed Sun. ACTV: Sant' Angelo.

Osteria di Santa Marina €€€ *Campo Santa Marina, Castello 591, tel: 041-5285239.* Traditional and delightful inn with tables on the square in summer. Specialises in creative seafood cuisine based on Venetian classics. Closed Sun and Mon. ACTV: Rialto.

Rosticerria San Bartolomeo € *Calle della Bissa 5424 San Marco, tel: 041-5223569.* This place displays delicious food, which is served at a fast counter on the ground floor or, for slightly more money, in a restaurant section upstairs. It tends to be packed except for off-peak hours. Take-aways available. ACTV: Rialto.

Terrazza Goldoni €€–€€€€ *Calle Goldoni 4488, San Marco, tel: 041-5224168.* With a garden terrace (heated in winter) just beyond the San Marco gondola moorings, this is an elegant place, which often has live music. The fixed-price menus are good value. Look out for the delicious special house soufflé dessert. ACTV: Rialto.

Trattoria da Remigio €€€ *Salizzada dei Greci, Castello 3416, tel: 041-5230089.* A simple indoor trattoria that is popular with the locals. Try the gnocchi and any one of the many fish specials. Closed Mon evening and Tues. ACTV: San Zaccaria.

DORSODURO, SAN POLO AND SANTA CROCE

Ai Gondolieri €€€€ *Ponte del Formager, San Vio, Dorsoduro 36, tel: 041-5286396.* This restaurant has a stylish, modern dining room where some of the best meat and vegetables in Venice are prepared, *nouvelle-cuisine* style. Try the stuffed courgettes (zucchini). Note that they don't do fish. Closed Tues. ACTV: Accademia.

Alla Madonna €–€€€ *Calle della Madonna, San Polo 594, tel: 041-5223824.* Venice's most famous medium-priced fish restaurant is a maze of beamed and stuccoed rooms and it caters for a variety of tastes—visitors, locals, students and business people alike congregate here. Closed Wed. ACTV: Rialto.

Alla Zucca €–€€ *Ponte del Megio, off Campo San Giacomo dell'Orio, Santa Croce 1762, tel: 041-5241570.* This small, modern place offers a pleasant, relaxed atmosphere. The daily changing menu is strong on pasta and inventive vegetable dishes but there are also meat dishes and excellent desserts. Dine outside beside a small canal in summer. Closed Sun. ACTV: San Stae.

Antica Trattoria Poste Vecchie €€€ *Pescaria, San Polo 1608, tel: 041-721822.* The city's oldest restaurant, located near the fish market, is a warren of tiny atmospheric rooms, some dating back to the 16th century. Fish dominates the menu. Closed Tues. ACTV: Rialto.

Collezione Peggy Guggenheim Café €–€€ *Dorsoduro 701, tel: 041-2405411.* With a menu of salads, soups, pasta and fish created by nearby Ai Gondolieri's chef, this is a gem if you're visiting the museum. Desserts are fabulous. Open for lunch only; closed Tues. ACTV: Accademia or Salute.

La Bitta €€ *Calle Lunga San Barnaba, Dorsoduro 2753A, tel: 041-5230531.* Informal little restaurant which serves almost entirely meat. Good value and popular with the locals. Closed Sun. ACTV: Ca' Rezzonico.

La Furatola €€€–€€€€ *Calle Lunga San Barnaba 2870A, tel: 041-5208294.* A cosy place that is famous for its fresh fish. The ample portions of pasta are often big enough to share. Fabulous desserts. Closed Mon lunch, Wed, Thurs and Aug. ACTV: Ca' Rezzonico.

Locanda Montin €€–€€€ *Fondamenta di Borgo, San Trovaso, Dorsoduro 1147, tel: 041-5227151.* The food at Locanda Montin draws mixed reviews and a little too much is made of the restaurant's history – it was once a haunt for artists and writers. However, the lovely garden can't be faulted. Closed Wed. ACTV: Ca' Rezzonico.

Osteria Da Fiore €€€€ *Calle del Scaleter 2202, San Polo, tel: 041-721308.* Simplicity, top-quality food and the inimitable skills of chef Maria Martin have gained this elegant, rather formal little place rave reviews from international food critics. Closed Sun, Mon and Aug. ACTV: San Stae.

Pizzeria ae Oche € *Calle del Tintor 1552, Santa Croce, tel: 041-5241161.* This informal place offers an incredible range of excellent pizzas in unpretentious surroundings – hence the frequent queues. Closed Mon. ACTV: San Stae.

Riviera €€€ *Zattere, 1473 Dorsoduro, tel: 041-5227621.* With outdoor seating overlooking the wide Giudecca Canal, the stylish Riviera is famous for exquisite homemade pasta and very fresh fish and seafood. Closed Mon. ACTV: San Basilio.

Taverna San Trovaso €–€€ *Fondamenta Priuli, Dorsoduro 1016, tel: 041-5203703.* This friendly pizzeria/trattoria is popular with the locals, especially with families. Book a table downstairs in the brick-vaulted room. Portions are large, even on the good-value *menù turistico*. Closed Mon. ACTV: Accademia.

GIUDECCA

Harry's Dolci €€€–€€€€ *Fondamenta San Biagio, Giudecca 773, tel: 041-5224844.* Shares its management and a gourmet menu with Harry's Bar *(see page 139)*, but slightly less expensive and has sweeping views of Venice across the Giudecca Canal. Off hours it's popular for the divine desserts. Closed Tues; Nov–mid-Mar. ACTV: Palanca.

THE ISLANDS

Ai Pescatori €€–€€€ *Piazza Galuppi, Burano, tel: 041-730650.* The excellent, family-owned Ai Pescatori is supplied with fresh fish by the island's fishermen. Great *moleche fritte* or *anguilla alla buranese*. Open for lunch; dinner by reservation. Closed Wed.

La Torre al Buso €€–€€€ *Campo Santo Stefano, Murano, tel: 041-739662.* Good seafood served at fabulous tables beside the water. Packed on weekends. Lunch only.

Locanda Cipriani €€€€ *Piazza Santa Fosca 29, Torcello, tel: 041-730150.* Idyllic, rustic spot renowned for its cuisine. Simple, classic dishes such as *carpaccio cipriani*, fish grills and *risotto alla Torcellano*, with lagoon vegetables and herbs. Reservations essential. Closed Tues; and Jan.

INDEX